PREPARING FOR A CAREER IN MEDIA AND DESIGN

PREPARING FOR A CAREER IN MEDIA AND DESIGN

Steven Carniol

Director of Education
Academic Dean, Lincoln College
Adjunct Assistant Professor,
Long Island University,
C. W. Post Campus

Upper Saddle River, New Jersey
Columbus, Ohio

Library of Congress Cataloging-in-Publication Data

Carniol, Steven.
    Preparing for a career in media and design / Steven Carniol.—1st ed.
        p. cm.
    Includes bibliographical references and index.
    ISBN-13: 978-0-13-228888-0
    1. Graphic arts—Vocational guidance.   2. Commercial art—Vocational guidance.   I. Title.
    NC1001. C375 2008
    741. 6023—dc22

                                                                                            2007050466

Editor in Chief: Vernon Anthony
Acquisitions Editor: Gary Bauer
Senior Managing Editor: JoEllen Gohr
Editorial Assistant: Kathleen Rowland
Project Manager: Christina Taylor
Production Coordination: S4Carlisle Publishing Services
Design Coordinator: Diane L. Ernsberger
Cover Designer: Ali Mohrman
Operations Specialist: Pat Tonneman
Director of Marketing: David Gesell
Marketing Manager: Leigh Ann Sims
Marketing Assistant: Les Roberts

This book was set in New Baskerville by S4 Carlisle Publishing Services. It was printed and bound by Edwards Brothers, Ann Arbor, MI. The cover was printed by Phoenix Color Corp.

Pearson Education Ltd.
Pearson Education Singapore Pte. Ltd.
Pearson Education Canada, Ltd.
Pearson Education—Japan

Pearson Education Australia Pty. Limited
Pearson Education North Asia Ltd.
Pearson Educación de Mexico, S.A. de C.V.
Pearson Education Malaysia Pte. Ltd.

10 9 8 7 6 5 4 3 2 1
ISBN-13: 978-0-13-228888-0
ISBN-10:   0-13-228888-5

CONTENTS

PREFACE

As a former Assistant Professor instructing classes in Career Development for media and design students and now as an Academic Dean, I have noticed that students are learning the technical and design skills necessary to enter the field but do not know how to start their careers. Students do not know what to include in their portfolio or how to write a resume, draft cover letters, or prepare and conduct themselves in a job interview. They do not understand employee benefits, 401(k) plans, and health insurance plans offered through employers—or how to be part of a team working together to meet a deadline.

Students also lack a practical understanding of what it means to work as a freelancer. Many professionals in media and design careers work as freelancers or have full-time jobs and freelance on the side. This book explores how to start your own freelance business, how to negotiate a contract, and how to protect your creative work. Having also worked as a freelance Audio Engineer, Web Designer, and Multimedia Designer, I share many of my experiences of how to work with clients, price your time, and market yourself.

Throughout the course of my professional and teaching career I have developed comprehensive lessons that focus on skills necessary for students to achieve professional success. This book is a compilation of these lessons with a proven track record at preparing students to enter the workforce or advance their careers. Organized as a step-building process, this book uses clear and concise language to prepare the reader for a new profession. Whether you are new to the workforce or are looking to change careers, this book will help you prepare for and adapt to your new field.

Use this book as a starting point for your new career journey. In addition to this textbook, visit the associated website, www.prenhall.com/carniol. You will find the supplemental material for this text, further discussions on the topics presented in this book, and tips for writing cover letters and resumes, creating portfolios, and negotiating a fair salary.

You can also contact me directly from the contact link on the website or at Steven@careercrib.com. I will be more than happy to answer any questions you may have and help you start your journey. You may also send me links to your digital portfolio or demo reels for possible inclusion in the website.

As you start or advance your career, I am confident that you will find this book useful. I wish you the best of luck in your career in media and design!

ACKNOWLEDGMENTS

I would like to extend my gratitude to the many people who helped make this book happen. First, I would like to thank all of my former students from the Katharine Gibbs School and C.W. Post University: Your quest for knowledge and desire to be prepared for the real world inspired me to develop this book. Next, I would like to thank my former professors at C.W. Post University: Andrea Urist for pushing me and guiding me through the learning process, and Patrick Aievoli for being a mentor, advisor, and supporter. I would also like to thank my colleagues Rob Doran and Max Dutton for giving me the writing bug. I would like to express my appreciation to my Acquisitions Editor, Gary Bauer of Prentice Hall, for his guidance and patience throughout the writing process and taking a chance on a first-time author. I would also like to express my appreciation to Dr. Carl Bridges at Lincoln Educational Services, for seeing my potential and giving me the opportunity to advance my career.

I would also like to thank Brooke Hunter-Lombardi of Columbus College of Art & Design, Dr. Joan Stone and Donna C. Cullen of Rochester Institute of Technology, Katie English of AIGA, Gerri Michael Dyer of the Agency for Healthcare Research and Quality, Richard Stim of Nolo.com, and Kristen Puttagio, Freelance Illustrator, for their contributions to this book.

Finally, I would like to thank my family for their love and support. This book is also in loving memory of Louis Chaiet and Diane and David Carniol, who would have loved to see this book published.

ONLINE INSTRUCTOR'S RESOURCES

Register today at www.prenhall.com to access instructor resources digitally.

To access supplementary materials online, instructors need to request an instructor access code. Go to **www.prenhall.com**, click the **Instructor Resource Center** link, and then click **Register Today** for an instructor access code. Within 48 hours after registering you will receive a confirming e-mail including an instructor access code. Once you have received your code, go to the site and log on for full instructions on downloading the materials you wish to use.

CHAPTER 1

Starting Your New Career Path

OUTLINE

1.1 Internships
1.2 Starting a Career Path
1.3 Career Planning Worksheet

OBJECTIVES

- Review the introduction to the book
- Identify the importance of an internship
- Prepare for your internship
- Planning your career path
- Create a plan to obtain your ideal job

INTRODUCTION

Choosing a new career path is always challenging, especially when entering the world of media and design. This book is designed to give you the necessary tools to successfully start your new journey. Up until this point you have probably been working hard to learn design skills and master current industry software. You will need these skills to enter the field, but starting a career and entering the workforce is a skill in itself. In fact, many of the topics covered in this book are *life skills* that will transcend the career you choose to pursue now and will help you throughout your life as your career travels down different paths. As you take your first steps toward becoming an industry professional, this book will explore the following topics:

- Building a resume
- Developing a portfolio
- Searching for jobs
- Writing a cover letter
- Mastering interview techniques
- Negotiating salary and benefits
- Understanding benefits
- Working freelance
- Protecting your creative property (copyrighting)

1.1 INTERNSHIPS

Completing an internship is an important part of your educational experience. There is a lot more to your education than just the technical and design skills you learn in school. Working in the field as an intern will give you firsthand experience and allow you to test out your new skills.

1.1.1 Why Do Employers Hire Interns?

Employers hire interns knowing that they have not worked in the field before; therefore, they expect the interns to work for their company for a limited time to gain experience in the field. Most interns are not paid; when they are, it is usually only a small stipend. As the internship is considered part of the educational process, employers take in interns because they provide extra help in their firms with little or no cost. Since most internships are arranged through a school and are for college credit, the employer is not responsible for taxes and insurance that are associated with hiring employees.

In addition to the inexpensive labor, employers get a chance to work with interns for a limited time and see what type of workers they are. Often, internships can lead to entry-level jobs if the company has vacancies. Interns who have proven themselves are in a much better position to obtain an entry-level position with the company than somebody who the employer has not worked with before. Make sure to take your internship seriously and work as hard as you can. At a minimum you should walk away from your internship with a positive learning experience, a letter of reference, networking contacts, and a better understanding of the industry.

1.1.2 Maximizing Your Internship Experience

You may have mastered your technical and design skills at school, but working in the field is much more involved than just being an expert in your software of choice. Learning how to work with clients, collaborate with co-workers, and meet contractual deadlines is as important as your design skills. It is not enough to be a strong designer; you need to be reliable and easy to work with, possess strong communication skills, demonstrate flexibility, and be enthusiastic.

One of the biggest mistakes students make is not taking their internship seriously. Often, students view the internship as a nuisance and something they just have to get through before they can apply for a *"real job"* in the field. Do not make this mistake! Your internship is a real job and probably your first experience in the field at a commercial facility. Although you may have already started freelancing and may even be making good money with your freelance work, this is a chance to see how a larger company functions.

Interns often do a lot of the busy work in the office such as making photocopies, answering phones, and moving boxes around. Most jobs require many of the same tedious tasks. A proper internship will also allow you to get involved in some type of professional project. However, do not expect to be the project's lead designer. Instead, the intern will often handle basic duties associated with the project. Remember, you are there to watch and learn in addition to gaining some hands-on experience. Regardless of the task, demonstrate a high level of enthusiasm for the task you are assigned. Do not complain! As you demonstrate your competency and willingness to accept all duties assigned, you will be given greater responsibility. This is true of any job. Think of it from the employer's point of view: Would you let an intern, still in college, lead a large client's project? Do not expect the employer to, either. They will, however, let you get involved and give you increased responsibility as your working relationship grows.

Be ambitious, not a nuisance!

As an intern it is important to demonstrate your desire to succeed. Here are some tips to help you thrive during your internship:

- **Show up on time.** Your punctuality is essential to making a good impression. Your employer will report your punctuality on your internship evaluation report. Your punctuality will also affect whether or not the employer will write you a letter of recommendation.

- **Demonstrate enthusiasm for your job.** Whatever the task, tackle it with the same enthusiasm as you would a lead assignment.

- **Accept your job assignments with a positive attitude.** For example, while working on a TV set you may be asked to wrap up all the cables at the end of a shoot. This might not be the most exciting part of television production, but it needs to be done. Just smile and complete the task efficiently.

- **Be courteous to all employees.** From the company CEO to the secretary and the janitor, treat everybody with respect. The way you treat other people is a reflection on you. Your supervisor will take notice.

- **Ask for more work.** Many interns only do what they are told and cannot wait for their shift to end. Stand out! When work is slow, ask for additional assignments.

- **Network.** Introduce yourself to as many employees at the company as you can. Make sure you take advantage of your new professional environment. Let them see what a hard-working intern you are.

- **Do not complain.** Many of the assignments you will be given are not glamorous jobs, but somebody has to do them.

- **Do not ask questions that do not relate to an assignment when working in front of clients.** Being new to the field, you may have many questions. It is OK to want to learn and ask questions; just pick the appropriate time to ask them. If you have a question that is relevant to an assignment you are working on, use your best judgment of whether or not it is appropriate to ask the question with the client present. If you have a question because you are curious about something new you are seeing, save it for after the clients leave. *Do not second guess your supervisor in front of the client.*

- **Unless you are asked, keep your opinion to yourself.** Too often, interns may suggest a design idea or comment on something they do not like. For example, you may not like the color choices for a particular brochure, but the designer may be locked into the color choices because of the client's specifications. Most employers will ask you for your opinion; just wait for the appropriate time. You may also ask your employer when you are first hired as an intern if it is OK to share your ideas. If they say yes, ask when would be the most suitable time to share your ideas.

1.2 STARTING A CAREER PATH

Although you have chosen the field you want to pursue, starting your career path can seem like a difficult task. Most graduates have skills that would apply to multiple positions. You probably have picked out your dream job and are working toward it, but you need to establish yourself and build a work history that will make you a strong candidate for your dream position. You need to research the type of qualifications necessary to land your dream job. Use the career planning worksheet (Figure 1–4) at the end of this chapter to help you plan you career path. A good place to start is to search for job leads and job descriptions that apply to that job. For example, if your career goal is to become a Senior Art Director, then search out those positions and look for the job qualifications employers are seeking. A job advertisement for a Senior Art Director may say:

> *Seeking Senior Art Director for a growing advertising agency with a minimum of six years of agency experience and a portfolio of large commercial clients. Must have experience in both print and Web marketing. A strong sense of design and the ability to work in a fast-paced, task-oriented environment is a must.*

Obviously, you are not going to obtain this position as a new graduate from college. However, if this is the type of position you are seeking, then you need a plan to get the required experience. Although this particular job may not be available when you are ready for the position, others with similar requirements will be.

In planning toward obtaining this type of position, you would want to seek out an entry-level job at a large advertising agency. If this means accepting less pay to work at the larger firm, then that is a sacrifice you need to consider. Remember your goal: You want to be a Senior Art Director. You would also want to look at the agency's client list. Most companies will list some of their larger clients as part of their marketing material, as well as on their website. Again, you are looking for a company that has large clients.

If a position at a large firm is not available, then you should seek an entry-level job at a smaller firm within the same field. One advantage of working at a smaller firm is you will probably have greater responsibilities assigned to you and have the ability to contribute more on projects. Use the experience from the smaller firm to help you obtain a position at the larger firm. As you build experience and a portfolio with the smaller company, you will be more attractive to the larger firms. Another thing to consider is you might actually like working for the smaller firm, which may be in a growth phase. After all, most large companies started out as small businesses at one point. You may have a job with the next rapidly growing agency, which can work to your advantage. Once you are with the company, you will get a good pulse for where they are headed.

1.2.1 What Are My Career Options?

Is the career you are choosing a viable career? Will you be able to support yourself and possibly a family? These are important questions when mapping out a career path. (*Salary research and information is covered in Chapter 7 of this book.*) In addition to reviewing regional salary information, industry publications are also a good place to start your research. The following charts and graphs in Figures 1–1, 1–2 and 1–3 are reprinted with permission from the "AIGA ‖ Aquent Survey of Design Salaries 2007" report. For the latest salary and job description information from AIGA, visit their website at: *http://www.designsalaries.com/*.

REVIEW QUESTIONS/ACTIVITIES

1. Describe the benefits of completing an internship. How can this help somebody obtain a job?
2. List three things that you should not do as an intern.
3. List five tips that will help you succeed as on intern.
4. Describe your dream job. Based upon the Career Planning Worksheet, what areas do you need to improve upon to reach this goal?

Median total cash compensation 2000–2007

POSITION	2000	2001	2002	2003	2004	2005	2006*	2007	ANN. RATE
Consumer Price Index inflation		2.2%	2.7%	1.4%	2.2%	2.6%	3.4%	3.2%	
Solo designer	$52,000	$60,000	$56,000	$55,000	$55,000	$60,000	$49,000	$60,000	2.0%
% change from prior year:		15.4%	-6.7%	-1.8%	0.0%	9.1%	-18.3%	22.4%	
Owner, Partner, Principal	100,000	100,000	100,000	93,000	100,000	100,000	80,000	113,000	1.7%
		0.0%	0.0%	-7.0%	7.5%	0.0%	-20.0%	41.3%	
Creative/Design director	85,000	84,000	85,000	85,000	85,000	90,000	80,000	98,600	2.1%
		-1.2%	1.2%	0.0%	0.0%	5.9%	-11.1%	23.3%	
Art director	55,000	62,500	62,000	60,000	65,000	65,000	60,900	72,000	3.8%
		13.6%	-0.8%	-3.2%	8.3%	0.0%	-6.3%	18.2%	
Senior designer	52,300	54,000	53,000	55,000	55,000	56,000	52,000	62,000	2.4%
		3.3%	-1.9%	3.8%	0.0%	1.8%	-7.1%	19.2%	
Designer	38,000	40,000	40,000	40,000	41,200	42,500	39,800	45,000	2.4%
		5.3%	0.0%	0.0%	3.0%	3.2%	-6.4%	13.1%	
Entry-level designer		31,000	32,000	30,000	31,000	32,000	33,000	35,000	2.0%
			3.2%	-6.3%	3.3%	3.2%	3.1%	6.1%	
Print production artist	35,000	38,000	40,000	40,000	40,000	40,000	40,000	44,800	3.5%
		8.6%	5.3%	0.0%	0.0%	0.0%	0.0%	12.0%	
Web designer	45,000	52,000	50,000	50,000	50,000	52,000	48,000	55,000	2.9%
		15.6%	-3.8%	0.0%	0.0%	4.0%	-7.7%	14.6%	
Copywriter	44,800	50,000	54,000	58,000	58,000	55,000	65,000	62,000	4.6%
		11.6%	8.0%	7.4%	0.0%	-5.2%	18.2%	-4.6%	
Print production manager	50,000	48,000	50,000	52,000	52,500	55,000		62,000	3.1%
		-4.0%	4.2%	4.0%	1.0%	4.8%			
Marketing/New business manager or director				70,000	75,000	75,000	62,500	80,000	3.3%
					7.1%	0.0%	-16.7%	28.0%	
Web developer (front end/interface systems)	51,400	55,000	58,200	50,000	55,000	60,000	60,000	60,000	2.2%
		7.0%	5.8%	-14.1%	10.0%	9.1%	0.0%	0.0%	
Web programmer/Developer (back end systems)	67,500	65,000	62,900	56,000	56,000	60,600		65,000	-0.5%
		-3.7%	-3.2%	-11.0%	0.0%	8.2%			
Web producer/Senior producer/ Executive producer	65,000	69,000	75,000	65,000	65,000	70,000	54,100	75,000	2.0%
		6.2%	8.7%	-13.3%	0.0%	7.7%	-22.7%	38.6%	
Content developer	47,000	47,500	50,000	46,500	55,000	65,000	70,500	58,800	3.2%
		1.1%	5.3%	-7.0%	18.3%	18.2%	8.5%	-16.6%	

*NOTE: Change in 2006 survey methodology may have affected measurements.

FIGURE 1-1 Median total cash compensation 2000–2007
Source: Aquent Survey of Design Salaries 2007. © AIGA

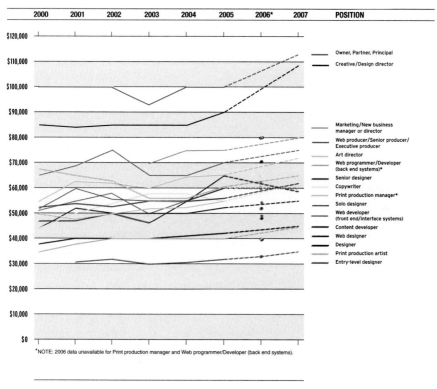

A NOTE ON THE 2006 METHODOLOGY
In 2006, a different research methodology was used that may have underestimated income. The 2006 data are reflected by dots and excluded from the trend line; the trend line from 2005 through the most recent data is reflected by a dotted line. The 2007 data are based on the same methodology as all previous years except 2006.

Median total cash compensation   2000–2007   I 7

FIGURE 1–2   Median total cash compensation 2000–2007
Source: Aquent Survey of Design Salaries 2007. © AIGA

Compensation overview

	SALARY/WAGES			SALARY/WAGE COMPARISON	TOTAL COMPENSATION			RESPONDENTS
	25th%	MEDIAN	75th%		25th%	MEDIAN	75th%	
Solo designer	$40,000	$ 60,000	$80,000	━╺╋╸━	$ 42,000	$60,000	$80,300	926
Owner, Partner, Principal	65,000	100,000	145,000	━━━╋╺━━━	72,000	113,000	175,000	611
Creative/Design director	73,000	90,000	116,000	━╺╋╸━━	75,000	98,600	130,000	945
Art director	55,000	70,000	82,000	━╋╸	60,000	72,000	90,000	1047
Senior designer	50,000	60,000	70,000	◄╋╸	50,000	62,000	75,000	1,423
Designer	37,500	44,000	52,000	◄╋╸	39,000	45,000	55,000	1,621
Entry-level designer	30,000	35,000	40,000	◄╋╸	31,000	35,000	40,000	749
Print production artist	35,000	41,200	50,000	━╋╸	36,500	44,800	53,000	419
Web designer	45,000	54,000	65,000	◄╋╸	46,000	55,000	70,000	390
Copywriter	45,000	60,000	72,000	━╺╋╸━	48,000	62,000	77,000	340
Print production manager	50,000	60,000	70,000	◄╋╸	50,000	62,000	76,000	418
Marketing/New business manager or director	52,000	75,000	90,000	━━╋╺━	57,000	80,000	100,000	292
Web developer (front end/interface systems)	48,000	60,000	72,000	◄╋╸	50,000	60,000	75,000	204
Web programmer/Developer (back end systems)	52,000	60,000	75,000	◄╋╸	54,000	65,000	80,000	131
Web producer/Senior producer/ Executive producer	60,000	70,000	80,000	◄╋╸	60,000	75,000	84,000	121
Content developer	45,000	55,000	65,000	◄╋╸	45,000	58,800	72,500	83

FIGURE 1-3   Compensation overivew
Source: Aquent Survey of Design Salaries 2007. © AIGA

CAREER PLANNING WORKSHEET

Use this worksheet to help plan your career path. The purpose of this worksheet is to help identify what skills and experience you have and will need to land your ideal job.

Job Title: _____

Job Description: _____

_____

_____

_____

_____

Education Analysis

Required Education	Current Education Completed	Additional Education Needed
Bachelor of Arts Major: Graphic Arts	Associate of Applied Science Major: Graphic Design	Two years (60 credits) to complete Bachelor's Degree

List possible methods to obtain education required for your ideal job:

1. *i.e.: Pursue online Bachelor's degree while working in field.* _____

2. _____

3. _____

4. _____

5. _____

Experience Analysis

Required Experience Job requirements	Related Experience List experience you possess	Needed Experience List experience you need to acquire
Four years print and Web design experience	Two years Web design experience	Two years more Web design Four years print

List possible methods to obtain missing experience required for your ideal job:

1. _____
2. _____
3. _____
4. _____
5. _____

Skills Analysis

Required Skills *Job requirements*	Related Skills *List skills you possess*	Needed Skills *List skills you need to acquire*
Advanced Photoshop skills	Moderate Photoshop skills	Additional Photoshop training

List possible methods to obtain missing skills required for your ideal job:

1. _____
2. _____
3. _____
4. _____
5. _____

List possible job titles that will help you reach your career goals:

1. _____
2. _____
3. _____
4. _____
5. _____

Summarize your career path plan. In addition to describing your goals, create a timeframe to complete each milestone:

	Goal	Description/ Purpose	Target Date of Completion	Date Completed
1				
2				
3				
4				
5				
6				
7				
8				

_____
_____
_____
_____
_____
_____

FIGURE 1-4 Career planning worksheet

Writing the Perfect Resume

OUTLINE

OBJECTIVES

- Learn the importance of effective resume writing
- Learn how to format your resume
- Identify what information to include in a resume
- Develop an effective resume presentation

INTRODUCTION

A well-written resume is the key to obtaining an interview. You can be the most qualified person for a position, but if your resume is not written well, the employer will skip right over it. In fact, as a recent graduate in the media and design field, your resume is the first creative design a potential employer will see. Use it to show the employer you understand design and presentation. Present your information in an organized, precise presentation that will catch an employer's attention.

An employer searching for new talent can be overwhelmed with applicants. Employers may receive hundreds of resumes and sifting through them is a daunting task to say the least. Your resume must catch the employer's eye from the first glance. The employer will separate the resumes of interest for further consideration. Often the employer will be inducted with the applicant. In fact, your cover letter may never be read if your resume does not present well. So it is important to put your best effort into both documents. *Surviving the initial screening process may be the hardest stage in applying for a job.* Once you survive the initial screening process, your resume and cover letter will receive serious consideration and you may be called in for an interview.

2.1 MARKETING YOURSELF

Think of your resume as an advertisement of what you have to offer. Think of yourself as a product that will fill a company's needs and your resume as your press kit. Ask yourself: If you were the employer, what would you be looking for? You want to highlight these items in your resume. Often, you will have to customize your resume for a particular job. Analyze the employer's needs and present your resume as a solution to their vacancy.

2.2 RESUME FORMATS

Chronological: The chronological resume highlights your work experience. It may be most suitable for a professional in a traditional line of employment. If you have an extensive background in your field with a job history of well-known companies, this may be the format to choose. In this format, your skills and accomplishments are listed under the corresponding job title. If you want to draw attention to your skills and accomplishments, it may be more appropriate to choose the functional or combination resume format.

Functional: A functional resume highlights your skills and accomplishments in individual categories. Listing the skills and accomplishments separate from your employment history will help connect your assets to the job you are applying for. This format may be most appropriate for new graduating students, people changing careers, or people seeking any position that requires specific skills and training.

As a student entering the media and design fields, this resume format may give you the most flexibility to focus your resume to your new career. The functional resume will allow you to tell the employer about your specific skills and software knowledge.

Combination: You may choose to combine both formats. A combined format still lists your skills and accomplishments; however, you can list your accomplishments under the heading of each specific job.

See Figures 2–1, 2–2, & 2–3 at the end of this Chapter to review resume samples.

GENERAL RESUME TIPS

- **Organization**—Present your information in a well-organized manner. Make sure your important information is easy to find. A potential employer is not going to search for hidden gems of information.

- **Proofreading**—Make sure to check your resume for spelling, punctuation, and grammatical mistakes.

- **Be precise**—Do not make your resume wordy. List the information in exact wording that is clear and to the point.

- **Language**—Use industry terms to demonstrate knowledge of the industry, but do not show off.

- **Targeting the job**—Make sure your resume is presented in a manner that will address the employer's needs.

- **Paper choice**—If you are mailing your resume, use a high-quality paper. Papers that are made with cotton fibers and (or) a watermark present well. If you are using watermarked paper, make sure to print your resume so that the watermark reads properly. Yes, the employer may check this and it shows you pay attention to detail.

E-MAILED RESUMES

If e-mailing, you are best off sending your resume as an attached PDF file. If you send a specific application file such as a Microsoft Word or a Word Perfect file, the employer may not be able to open it. Additionally, PDF files will keep all formatting and font information intact, ensuring proper presentation of your resume. The only exception is if the employer requests a specific file format.

2.3 RESUME CONTENT

Header and Contact Information: Include all important contact information. Use your legal name, mailing address, phone number(s), and e-mail address.

Notes:

- **Phone number.** You may wish to include a day-time number, evening number, and a cell phone number. Make sure the phone number you list has the ability to take messages.
- **E-mail.** Your e-mail address is very important. Avoid using cute names that only your friends get. Choose an e-mail address that is professional. You may want to create a new e-mail account just for job searching. Yahoo.com, Hotmail.com, and Gmail.com offer free e-mail accounts.

Objective: Although it may be the most difficult part of your resume to write, the objective is useful in focusing your resume to your desired career. It lets an employer know exactly what career path you are pursuing. It also lets the employer know if you are a strong fit for the open position. You will often need to customize your objective to the particular job that you are applying for.

Let's say you are applying for an entry-level Junior Designer position. The advertisement states, "Seeking an entry-level Junior Designer to assist in developing marketing material and website content for a commercial bank. Must be proficient in Photoshop, Illustrator, Quark, Dreamweaver, Flash, CSS, and HTML. Knowledge of Java Script a plus. The ideal candidate is highly organized, detail oriented, possesses strong communication skills, and is able to work as part of a team or independently to meet deadlines." Which of the following, objectives would get the employer's attention?

1. "Seeking a full-time graphic design position in which I can further develop my skills and expand my portfolio."
2. "Seeking an entry-level graphic design position in an organization that is in search of a highly motivated, proficient designer who

can contribute to the marketability and Web presence of a financial institution."

Obviously, the second choice is a better example of an objective, as it is important to directly address the needs of the company. Additionally, addressing the type of industry the company is in lets the employer know you are not just looking for the first job that comes your way; rather, you have a genuine interest of working in their industry.

Employers only care about what you are going to do for them. They are not interested in helping you develop your skills and portfolio so you can search for another job. They want to hire you to help the company improve its profitability. Yes, they want you to grow and improve, but mainly they want you to help their business grow. When drafting your objective, focus on the employer's needs, not your own.

Summary or Profile: You may choose to add a summary (or profile) section to your resume where you can list a few key traits that may help you stand out from the rest of the applicants. When including both an objective and summary on your resume, your objective should list your goals; the summary is a brief description of why you are a strong candidate. You may also incorporate your objective into your summary. When combining the objective in the summary, describe how your unique experience lends to your career goals. Items you may include in the summary are:

- A description of your expertise
- Awards, honors, and achievements
- A description of why your mix of experience is unique
- Personal traits and characteristics that lend to your professionalism

A strong summary will draw the attention of the reader and focus attention on your strongest attributes. The summary is more than a list of skills; it is a personal statement that lets you speak directly to the employer. In fact, the summary may entice the employer to actually take the time to read the cover letter.

Education: When listing your education, list your highest post-secondary degree achieved first. You should also list any additional certificate programs and training or software certification courses completed. Do not list your high school unless you attended a prestigious prep school or graduated from a special vocational program related to your field such as BOCES.

List the name of the institution, the school's location (city, state), full name of degree (do not use abbreviations such as BFA; state: Bachelor of

Fine Arts), major or area of concentration, GPA (if it is above a 3.5), and date (or expected date) of graduation. For example:

SUMMARY EXAMPLES

- Creative and highly motivated graphic designer with extensive Web and print design training. Especially strong traditional design background with an extensive still life and portrait portfolio, seeking a challenging entry-level Designer position with a company that values hard-working, task-oriented employees, willing to work long hours to meet the required deadlines.

- Photography graduate with extensive training in commercial photography, strong computer skills, and a great eye for composition. Over three years of wedding, portrait, and event photography experience in which most clients were obtained via referrals from previous clients. Excellent organizational and customer relations skills with the ability to make new client contacts and contribute to company growth.

- Highly trained, 3D animator specializing in character modeling, rigging, and texturing. Experienced in both 3d Studio Max and Maya. Acted as the lead character modeler for an advanced student project sponsored by the school's animation club. Also possess strong storyboarding skills and the ability to operate several nonlinear video editing systems including Avid and Final Cut Pro.

EDUCATION

Long Island University at C.W. Post Campus, Brookville, New York

Master of Arts

Major: Interactive Multimedia

GPA: 3.95

Graduation: June 2005

If you have credits from a college, but did not complete a degree at that school, you may list that school's information and the number of credits completed.

Other items to consider listing under the Education heading include

- List of high profile professors you may have studied under
- List of relevant course work if it is applicable to the position you are applying for
- Academic awards, scholarships, and fellowships as a listed item under the particular school. Alternately, you can create a separate section for awards and honors.

Skills: When entering a field that is often technical, outlining your skills is extremely important. Potential employers will look for this section to see if you are trained in the area of expertise they need. List your industry-related skills, application skills, and any other skills that may be valuable to an employer.

There are several ways to present the information in the skills section:

- Present the industry skill heading and then list subdivisions of that skill. List software knowledge under its own heading. For example:

DESIGN AND TECHNICAL SKILLS

3D Animation:	Subdivision Modeling, Character Animation, Texturing, Rigging, Low Polygon Animation
Video Production:	Nonlinear Video Editing, Compositing, 3 & 5 Point Lighting
Studio Art Skills:	Storyboarding, Figure Drawing, Still Life, Pastels, Pencil
Graphic Design:	Photo-Retouching, Pre-Flighting, Computer Illustration
Web Design:	HTML, CSS, Java Script, Web Animation, GIF Animation, Quicktime, and WMV File Optimization
Industry-Related Skills:	Sound Design and Editing, Loop Music Production, Script Writing, Story Development

SOFTWARE SKILLS

3D Animation:	3d Studio Max (with Character Studio), Maya, Strada
Video Production:	Avid, Final Cut Pro, Premiere, After Effects, Vegas Video, Encore, DVD Studio Pro

Graphic Design:	Photoshop, Illustrator, Quark, InDesign, Fireworks
Web Design:	Dreamweaver, Flash, Front Page
Audio:	Pro-Tools, Acid, Audition
Other:	Proficient in Mac and PC, MS Word, Excel

Another way to present your skills is to build your skills into a table or as bulleted items. For example:

SKILLS

Software

• Pro-Tools HD	• Acid Pro	• Sound Forge
• Adobe Audition	• Dreamweaver	• Sony Vegas Video
• Avid	• Flash	• Sony DVD Architect
• Final Cut Pro HD	• Illustrator	• Quark
• Adobe Photoshop	• Adobe ImageReady	• Proficient in Mac and PC

Technical, Production, and Design Skills

• Audio Recording and Mixing	• Sound Design and Editing	• Photo Retouching
• Audio Mastering	• A/V Post Production	• Nonlinear Digital Video Editing
• CD/DVD Authoring	• Photoshop Image Editing	• Compositing
• Web Design	• Color Correction	• HTML Coding

Accomplishments and Achievements: You may choose to add a section highlighting specific accomplishments that you are proud of. This section is optional, and it may be more appropriate to list your individual accomplishments under the specific job title, school attended, or volunteer work. Your accomplishment section can include the following types of accomplishments and achievements:

- Academic awards and acknowledgments
- Career and job-related achievements
- Volunteer and fundraising accomplishments
- Extracurricular leadership positions or participation
- Anything that you are proud of that an employer may see as a positive achievement

For example:

SELECTED ACCOMPLISHMENTS

- Coordinated Fundraiser for SADD (Students Against Drunk Driving); Raised $2,500 through donation drives and bake sales
- Recipient of 2004 Digital Art award sponsored by school's on-campus art magazine
- Provided volunteer peer tutoring in Digital Art Department
- Designed layout for class of 2005 yearbook

Experience: Although your in-field experience as a new college graduate may be limited, you should still list your past work experience. It is important to establish a work history regardless of what industry you were employed in. Employers know entry-level applicants may only have schooling and a possible internship within the industry. The highly motivated students may also have some freelance experience. However, it is important to establish that you have had a job before. Even a job at a fast food restaurant or a supermarket demonstrates work ethic and the ability to hold down a job.

Experience section guidelines

- List your work experience with your most recent job first. Your list should be compiled in reverse chronological order.
- Remember that more jobs is not necessarily best. Employers would rather see that you stayed in one position for a long time, rather than changing jobs every few months. Employees who leave after a short time are costly to a company, which must then advertise, interview, and train a new employee after you leave.

- When listing each job:
  - List the company name, location (city, state), and your employment start and end dates. Include the month and year, not just the year.
  - Include a one- or two-sentence description of the company, if desired.
  - List your job title.
  - Create a bulleted list describing your job duties, responsibilities, and accomplishments.
  - Do not write in the first person. Do not use the word "I" in your job description. Instead of writing, *"I edited and color corrected photos for publication,"* simply write, *"Edited and color corrected photos for publication."*

Example of how to list your experience:

EXPERIENCE

INNOVATIVE DESIGNS,   June 2005–Present
New York, New York
A graphic design firm specializing in print and Web design for individuals and businesses located in Manhattan.

Junior Graphic Designer

- Designed logos, flash animations, and packaging designs for clients as part of a design team
- Pre-Flight—Ensured that designs met printing specs for printers and that all images and fonts were packaged properly
- Verified client proofs and customer satisfaction
- Assisted Senior Designers with various tasks including layout design concept, research, file management, and project archiving

TARGET, Hicksville, New York   January 2003–June 2004

Discount Department Store

Cashier/Customer Service Representative

- Ensured customer satisfaction with services and products
- Operated register for check-out and customer returns
- Award: Employee of the Month—September 2003

Military Experience: If you have military experience, you should definitely list your service as its own heading. Employers will give you greater consideration. Not only have you served our country, but you understand the meaning of hard work. List the branch of military, rank, service dates, locations stationed, and a bulleted list of duties.

Awards and Honors: This optional section can be used to highlight any special recognition you may have received, although some of this information can also be listed under various headings. You may list the following items under this section or place it in the alternate sections listed in parentheses:

- Scholarships, Honor's List, Dean's List, President's List, Perfect Attendance awards, and other academic awards *(These items can also be listed under the Education section of your resume as a bulleted item under the associated school.)*

- Employee of the Month award and other job-related awards *(These items can also be listed under the appropriate job listing under Experience or under Accomplishments and Achievements.)*

- Civic, leadership, and community-related awards *(These items can also be listed under Accomplishments and Achievements.)*

- Art, Photography, Film, Film Festival, Animation, or any other creative awards *(These items can also be listed under Accomplishments and Achievements.)*

Publications: Any contributions you have made to a publication, either literary or artwork, should be listed under the heading Publications. Publication in any newspaper, magazine, books, or other mediums should be listed regardless of the size of the publication. When listing the items, list the name of the publication, date, issue number, and type of contribution you made.

Exhibitions: As someone starting a career in media and design, any public viewings that you have participated in can speak very highly for you. Exhibitions at locations from art galleries to local community centers should be listed. You can also include exhibitions at school. Include the location, date, title of the work, and nature of the work. You should also have a copy of the piece in your portfolio and digital portfolio.

Professional Organizations and Affiliations: As a graduating student and a new entry into the design and media fields, it is very important to join industry organizations. List all organizations that you are a member of. Since student discounts are available for most organizations, you should look for these discounted prices while you are still a student. Examples include: GAG (Graphic Artist Guild), AES (Audio Engineering Society), NATPE (National Association of Television Program Executives), and NAB (National Association of Broadcasters).

Interests and Hobbies: This optional section of your resume is not really necessary, but you might have some interesting things to add that do not fall under any of the previous categories. If you have hobbies or interests that might add to your marketability, list them here. Include physical activities such as jogging or martial arts. They show an employer that you take care of yourself and that you are less likely to take sick days. Be careful not to list things that make you sound like a couch potato or anything that might be perceived negatively.

2.4 ACTION AND POWER WORDS

Action and power words can help illustrate your positive traits. Use some of the following words to help make your resume stand out.

Accomplished	Collected	Drafted
Achieved	Communicated	Earned
Acquired	Compile	Edited
Adapted	Composed	Eliminated
Addressed	Computed	Enforced
Administered	Conducted	Established
Advised	Consolidated	Estimated
Analyzed	Constructed	Evaluated
Anticipated	Consulted	Examined
Arranged	Contracted	Expanded
Assembled	Converted	Experimented
Assessed	Coordinated	Explained
Assisted	Counseled	Fashioned
Attained	Created	Financed
Audited	Critiqued	Forecasted
Awarded	Defined	Formed
Broadened	Designed	Formulated
Budgeted	Detected	Founded
Built	Determined	Gathered
Calculated	Developed	Generated
Centralized	Devised	Grossed
Chaired	Diagnosed	Guided
Changed	Directed	Handled
Classified	Discovered	Hired
Coached	Displayed	Hypothesized
Collaborated	Doubled	Identified

Illustrated
Implemented
Improved
Increased
Influenced
Informed
Initiated
Inspected
Installed
Instituted
Instructed
Insured
Interpreted
Interviewed
Invented
Investigated
Joined
Led
Licensed
Launched
Learned
Lectured
Maintained
Managed
Marketed
Mediated
Minimized
Modeled
Monitored
Motivated
Negotiated
Networked
Obtained
Operated

Ordered
Organized
Oversaw
Performed
Persuaded
Photographed
Planned
Prepared
Presented
Printed
Processed
Produced
Produces
Programmed
Projected
Promoted
Proofread
Provided
Publicized
Published
Purchased
Qualified
Received
Recommended
Reconciled
Recorded
Recruited
Reduced
Referred
Refined
Rehabilitated
Reorganized
Repaired
Reported

Represented
Researched
Resolved
Responded
Restored
Retrieved
Reviewed
Revised
Scheduled
Selected
Set up
Simplified
Solved
Sorted
Studied
Summarized
Supervise
Supervised
Supplied
Surveyed
Taught
Tested
Trained
Transcribed
Translated
Traveled
Tutored
Upgraded
Used
Utilized
Won
Wrote

RESUME PREPARATION WORKSHEET

The following worksheet will help you gather the information needed to prepare a resume:

Personal and Contact Information:

Full Name: _____

Address: _____

_____

_____

Day time Phone Number: _____

Evening Phone Number: _____

E-mail: _____

Career Objective (Briefly describe your career goals for your next position): _____

_____

_____

Summary or Profile (Highlight your strongest marketable traits): _____

_____

_____

_____

Education: *List your highest degree achieved first:* _____

Name of School: _____

School's Location (City, State): _____

Degree (if completed. If not, list number of credits completed): _____

Major and Specializations: _____

_____

Graduation Date (Month/Year): _____

_____

Name of School: _____

School's Location (City, State): _____

Degree (if completed. If not, list number of credits completed):

_____

Major and Specializations: _____

_____

Graduation Date (Month/Year): _____

List related training including course work and training in addition to your degrees: _____

_____

_____

Skills:

Application Skills (List all computer applications including software such as word processing and spreadsheet design):

Applications	Skills Used Within Application	Skill Level (1–5)
Adobe Photoshop CS2	*Image Editing, Web Page Design, etc.*	*4*

Design, Technical, and Traditional Design Skills (List your skills that are related to your field):

Skill	Description (if applicable)	Skill Level (1–5)
Storyboarding	*Video and Film Preproduction*	*3*

Employment History (List your most recent job first):_____
Position Title: _____
Company: _____
Location (City, State): _____
Start Date (Month/Year): _____ End Date (Month/Year): _____
Description of Duties: _____

Position Title: _____
Company: _____
Location (City, State): _____

Start Date (Month/Year): _____ End Date (Month/Year): _____
Description of Duties: _____
_____

Military Experience (if applicable):
Branch of Military: _____
Rank: _____ Service Dates (Month/Year–Month/Year): _____
Locations Stationed: _____
Duties: _____
_____
_____

Industry Organization: _____
_____
_____

Awards and Honors: _____
_____
_____

Hobbies and Special Interests: _____
_____
_____
_____

FIGURE 2-1   Resume preparation worksheet

Melissa Smith

211 5th Avenue · Boston, MA 02331 · (415) 555–5555 · e-mail: M_Smith@Pratt.edu

OBJECTIVE

Seeking an entry-level design position in an organization that values highly creative, task-oriented designers, dedicated to increasing a company's marketability and web presence.

EDUCATION

Pratt Institute, Brooklyn, New York   May 2006
Bachelor of Fine Arts—Major: Communication Arts ~ GPA: 3.82
Honors: *Magna Cum Laude, National Honors Society*
Scholarships: *National Student Art Foundation, President's Academic Scholarship*

SKILLS

Applications and Computer Skills

- Adobe Photoshop
- Adobe Illustrator
- Adobe InDesign
- Adobe ImageReady
- Adobe After Effects
- Macromedia Dreamweaver
- Macromedia Director
- Macromedia Flash
- Macromedia Fireworks
- Quark Xpress
- Final Cut Pro
- Java Scripting, CSS
- HTML, XHTML, DHTML
- Action Scripting, Lingo
- Proficient in Mac and PC

Design and Technical Skills

- Web Design
- Web Master
- Interactive CD-ROM & DVD-ROM Authoring
- Digital Compositing
- Nonlinear Video Editing
- 2D Animation (Flash & Director)
- Photoshop Image Editing & Correcting
- Packaging Design
- Pre-Flighting
- Computer Illustration
- Typography
- Studio Art Skills

WORK EXPERIENCE

4/2004–Present
Freelance Graphic Designer; Boston, Massachusetts
- Design and maintain websites
- Design brand identity, logo, and promotional print material
- Create and implement Web and CD-ROM animations
- Work with clients to ensure the highest level of quality and client satisfaction

1/2006–5/2005
Brooklyn Press, Brooklyn, New York
Intern
- Assisted Art Director with advertisement layouts
- Designed promotional mailing fliers and internal newsletter
- Pre-Flighting: Assured all files were prepared properly for print

9/2003–5/2006
Pratt Institute; Brooklyn, New York
Work Study—Art Department
- Assisted Chairperson with clerical duties including filing, answering phones, and document preparation for department meetings
- Assisted professors with class preparation
- Tutored students in various design subjects and software

FIGURE 2-2   Melissa Smith

Jennifer Gonzales

3244 Harold Street
Los Angeles, CA 90008
(213) 555-9214
Jennyphoto@Careercrib.com

Objective: To obtain a photographer position with a publication in search of a highly motivated, creative artist dedicated to capturing imagery that exhibits realism and human emotion.

Summary: Photography graduate with extensive training in commercial photography, strong computer skills, and a great eye for composition. Over three years of wedding, portrait, and event photography experience in which most clients were obtained via referrals from previous clients. Excellent organizational and customer relations skills with the ability to make new client contacts and contribute to company growth.

Publications:
- **University Art Magazine**; Issue Date: January, 2004
  Featured photojournalism artist, "The Student From the Inside"
- **Modern Day Bride**; Issue Date: May, 2003
  Five-page spread, "Outdoor Weddings in Ohio"

Education:

Bachelor of Fine Arts—Photojournalism   May 2004
Ohio University, Athens, OH ~ GPA: 3.68 Cum Laude
Specialized Course-work: News Writing, Picture Editing, Photo Illustration, Photojournalism, Documentary/Essay, Information Gathering

Associate Degree in Applied Science—Graphic Design Dec 2001
Katharine Gibbs School, Melville, NY
Specialized Course-work: Typography, Computer Illustration, Web Design, Animation, Photo Concepts, Design Elements 2D, Design Elements 3D

Skills:	**– Computer Skills:** Photoshop, Illustrator, Flash, InDesign, Fireworks, Dreamweaver, Quark Xpress, MS Word, Excel, Proficient in Mac & PC
	– Photography: Digital, Film, Color Correction, Development, Lighting, Portrait, Photojournalism

---

Experience:	**Freelance Wedding Photographer**; Los Angeles, CA & Athens, OH
Jan. 01– Present	• Specializing in both traditional and photojournalism styles
	• Hired as a subcontractor by three different wedding photographers
	• Most business acquired through referrals and networking
	Assistant Photographer; Athens, Ohio
	Athens Daily
June 02– April 04	• Assisted Lead Photographers with on-location shoots
	• Performed image and color correction for print
	• Updated images on website • Archived all digital files from location shoots

---

Volunteer	**Boys and Girls Club of America,**	June 05
	Los Angeles, CA	
Experience:	Hosted photography workshop for at-risk youths	

Organizations:	Student Photographic Society (SPS), American Society of Media Photographers (ASMP)

FIGURE 2-3 Jennifer Gonzales

529 Riverside Road ~ San Diego, CA 92101 ~
(619) 555-1919 ~ JonSmith@Careercrib.com   **Jonathan Smith**

Career Objective:
:   Seeking an entry-level position with a Television Production team in search of a highly dedicated, task-oriented Production Assistant fully dedicated to meeting required deadlines while providing the highest level of skill and training.

Selected Accomplishments:
:   *Awards*

~ Young Filmmakers of America—2nd Place—Best Director—Documentary—2005 Student Film Festival
   ~ "The Grand Puba of the Frat House"—An inside look at Fraternity Leadership.
~ University of Southern California — Film Makers of the Future Grant — $10,000

Filmography

~ Documentary Film 2005—"The Grand Puba of the Frat House"—An inside look at Fraternity Leadership.
   ~ Producer, Director, and Editor
~ Dramatic Short 2004—"Instinctual Love"—15-minute drama about a woman and her desire to be loved by her emotionally disconnected parents. Director: Kimberly Jones
   ~ Lead Cameraperson, Editor, and Storyboard Artist
~ Comic Short 2004—"All I Want Is a Snack"—5-minute digital movie about one man's struggle to get his bag of potato chips that is stuck in a snack machine.
   ~ Producer, Director, Editor, Writer, Cameraperson, and Storyboard Artist

Education:

UNIVERSITY OF SOUTHERN CALIFORNIA,   May 2006
Los Angeles, CA
Bachelor of Arts—Cinema Television; Minor: Screenwriting
Relevant Course-work: Techniques in Motion Picture, Directing for Writers, Fundamentals of Cinematic Sound, Originating and Developing Ideas for Film, Directing for Television, The Cinematic Structure of a Scene, Advanced Multi-Camera Television Comedy Pilot, Directing the Composer, Special Effects in Cinema

Skills:

Software: Final Cut Pro, Avid, Media Composer, After Effects Professional, 3d Studio Max, Pro- Tools

Switchers and Decks: Panasonic AG-MX70SF, Sony DFS 700A, Sony DNV-5 Betacam

Cameras: Sony MSW-900, Panasonic AJ-SDC615, Sony DXC-D50L

Production: Nonlinear and Linear Editing, Screenwriting, Storyboarding, Directing, Advanced Compositing

Work Experience:

KNBC, Los Angeles, CA   Jan. 06–May 06
  Intern—Channel 4 News at 5
    • Set up newsroom before each broadcast
    • Archived broadcast master tapes and updated database
    • Tested ear prompt and teleprompt equipment before each broadcast
    • Assisted talent with various tasks

PRO VIDEO HOUSE, Los Angeles, CA   Sept. 04–Jan. 06
  Video Consultant—Professional Video Equipment retailer
    • Provided product knowledge and equipment training to customers
    • Advised customers on equipment recommendations and system configuration based upon needs and budget
    • Performed light equipment repairs and maintenance of equipment

FIGURE 2-4 Jonathan Smith

REVIEW QUESTIONS/ACTIVITIES

1. What is the difference between a chronological and functional resume? What type best fits your experience?

2. If you are new to a field and do not have any related work experience, should you list your work experience? Why or why not?

3. What file format should you use when e-mailing your resume?

CHAPTER 3

Your Portfolio

OBJECTIVES

- How to create a portfolio
- Present your best work
- Write an artist's statement
- How to photograph your work to create slides
- Know how to create a video demo reel

INTRODUCTION

In most industries, hiring decisions are made based upon your resume and interview. This is not the case in the media and design fields. If you are applying for a creative position, you will need to show a strong portfolio. Your resume will help get you an interview, but your portfolio will play a large role in landing the job.

Although you are most likely applying for an entry-level position, the employer will still request a portfolio. Ideally, it will contain a few professional projects that you may have completed as a freelancer while in school. However, even if your portfolio only consists of school projects you can still make a strong presentation. Hopefully, you have approached each school project as if it was a professional job and put your best effort forward. Either way, it is a good idea to review your work and decide if there are any final touches you can make to improve it.

Depending on your chosen field, the format of your portfolio will vary. Video and animation fields will require a demo reel. Graphic Designers, Traditional Artists, Photographers, and other non-motion-based visual artists will require a print portfolio and possibly slides. Web and multimedia designers will need to create a digital portfolio that can be delivered via the Internet and CD-ROM or DVD-ROM.

3.1 PRESENTATION

Regardless of the medium, your portfolio's presentation is just as important as its content. Your portfolio needs to be presented in a professional format. Traditional portfolios should be presented in a professional artist's portfolio. Each page should be mounted evenly and cleanly. Make sure that all edges of your artwork are cut straight and that there is no glue residue showing on the mounting. Use high quality prints on the appropriate paper (do not use standard 20 pound printer paper). Label each piece of artwork and describe what it is. If the project was created for school, label the class title and theme of the project. For more important pieces or for a series, you should create an artist's statement (see section 3.2).

Digital portfolios and demo reels presented on a VHS, CD, or DVD should be packaged professionally and creatively. Create a designed jewel case and CD label for your portfolio that includes your contact information. You would be surprised how important the packaging of your portfolio is to getting your material reviewed. Think about when you go to the video store to rent a movie. The first thing you look at is the cover of the movie. If you do not like the cover or see a star that you are familiar with, you are probably not going to read the back or ever rent the movie. You should put the same presentation effort into your portfolio's packaging as movie companies put into DVD packaging.

DIGITAL PORTFOLIO WARNING

One major issue with digital portfolios and demo reels is the CD-R or DVD-R often may not play in the employer's computer or DVD player. If your digital portfolio is designed for viewing on a computer, make sure your disc is cross-platform compatible. Test your portfolio or demo reel on both a Mac and a PC. Additionally, verify the place you are sending it to has a machine that can play the medium. Believe it or not, many people still do not have a computer that can read a DVD.

If you are presenting a video demo reel on DVD, make sure you have a VHS backup. Also ask in advance what medium the employer wants demo reels submitted on. Often a company will only accept demo reels that meet specific guidelines and predefined criteria. This information is often available on the company's website.

Your best option for creating a digital portfolio is to create a website. This will allow you to direct potential employers to your website when you e-mail your resume. Additionally, if your site is designed properly, you will not have to worry about the viewer being able to see your portfolio. Furthermore, this will also allow you to link your site to many other websites that have directories of portfolios or to allow your work to appear in search engines.

3.2 CREATING AN ARTIST'S STATEMENT

Creating an artist's statement can be challenging, but it is extremely important. Art galleries, employers, and other industry professionals expect to see an artist's statement accompanying your work.

Some may argue, "My work should speak for itself!" Yes, your artwork should speak for itself; however, the artist's statement will give the viewer a glimpse into your psyche. You should think of your statement as part of your work, not a separate document. It will help the viewer understand you and your art. It demonstrates thought and can argue your point of view. The statement will explain your personal connection with your art and make it a valid expression. It may also draw viewers to certain aspects of your art that they might not have noticed otherwise. Use the artist's statement to bring your creative work to a new level of understanding.

Artist's statements should be created regardless of the medium. Whether you work in oil paints, clay, or on commercial websites, there is still artist reasoning behind the design. This should be highlighted in the statement. If you are working on a commercial product, part of your statement may explain how the design is created around the need for easy navigation, current company logos, and the marketing needs.

3.2.1 Structuring Your Artist's Statement

One of the biggest mistakes you can make when drafting an artist's statement is rambling on too long. Most people will not read an entire statement if it is too long. Your statement is not your resume. Rather, it is a statement about a specific work or a series of pieces. When drafting your artist's statement, refer to the following guidelines (Figure 3–1):

- Your artist's statement should range between two to three short paragraphs. Keep the length to around 100 words.

- Use simple language. Make sure your artist's statement is easy to read and comprehensible for everybody. Using language that only a highly trained artist will understand may hurt your ability to land a job, sell a piece, or get your work shown in a gallery.

- Show your true self. Demonstrate your passion and emotion in your statement. This will help the viewer connect to your artwork.

- Do not predefine yourself. Although you should discuss the influences and styles you used during the creation of your work, do not label yourself as a _____ artist or compare your artwork to another artist. Use the Artist statement worksheet in Figure 3.1 as a tool for organizing & creating your Artist statement.

3.3 CREATING YOUR PORTFOLIO

Choosing the right pieces for your portfolio can be difficult. You may want to ask one of your professors or an industry professional for help selecting your best work. You want to choose the pieces that best demonstrate your strongest skills. Do not put work in your portfolio that you feel you need to explain. For example, suppose you created a website, but the client insisted that you use certain colors that do not work well together or asked you to use a font that is hard to read. If this is the case, do not use this piece. The worst thing you can do with your portfolio is fill it with work that you need to give explanations about. If you want to use something from a professional client, but you do not like something about it, fix it. Create a second version with your own creative choices for your portfolio. Just label it as a designer's proposal.

Keep your portfolio to a manageable size. You do not need to show every painting, sketch, photo, digital design, website, interactive presentation . . . well, you get the idea. Since your portfolio is a sampling of

ARTIST'S STATEMENT WORKSHEET

What mediums and techniques do you work in? _____

_____

_____

Why do you create your artwork? _____

_____

_____

_____

What do you hope to achieve with your artwork? _____

_____

_____

_____

Who are your influences and why? _____

_____

_____

_____

Why did you choose your color scheme? _____

_____

_____

_____

How do you choose your subjects? _____

_____

_____

_____

What is some of the feedback that you have received from people? _____

_____

_____

_____

What differentiates you from other artists? _____

_____

_____

_____

What is your education and formal art training? _____

_____

_____

_____

FIGURE 3-1   Artist's statement worksheet

your best work, you should aim for about fifteen to twenty creative works. At a minimum you should have at least ten creative works. Keep your portfolio to a size that can be viewed in a short time period. Since employers may be looking at hundreds of portfolios, they are not going to take the time to look at a portfolio that is too large. In fact, they have probably made a decision after reviewing the first four or five creative works. The rest of your portfolio is there to show that your designing sense is consistent and versatile.

When laying out your portfolio, put your best work first. You want to grab people's attention right away; it is also important to save a strong piece for the end. Remember to show some diversity. Do not show Fifteen pages of one website as your entire portfolio. Demonstrate that you are versatile and can design in many types of styles. For example, if you are a graphic designer specializing in print, you will want to include a broad range of print material such as corporate identity kits (letterhead, business card, envelope, and a possible brochure), book covers, newsletters, poster designs, CD or DVD designs, and magazine and newspaper advertisements.

Especially when you are new to a field, your work does not have to be for real companies. Create fictional companies and products to add projects to your portfolio. An even a better idea is to volunteer your services to friends, families, charities, and schools. By doing free work for a local charity or school, you are networking with local professionals. Often your volunteer work can lead to paying freelance jobs. It will also get exposure for your work and allow you to include published work in your portfolio. Additionally, the company will be more than happy to write you a letter of recommendation.

3.3.1 Traditional Portfolio

Your portfolio should contain up to twenty samples of your best work. You should have a minimum of ten to fifteen samples, but always choose quality over quantity. Include an informational sheet that highlights a description of each piece. Provide the title, medium, dimensions, and date completed of each sample work. In addition, include any press, reviews, awards, and exhibition information for your sample works.

Organizing your traditional portfolio

Now that you have selected your strongest pieces, you need to consider the order in which they are presented. Below you will find suggestions, but always remember that this is just a guide. We are talking about your personal body of work, and the selection and order should feel right to you.

1. **Wow!.** The first impression sets the tone. You should select one or two of your strongest pieces to begin your portfolio.

2. **Technical (everyone likes these).** The next few pieces should show off your abilities.

3. **Content.** The midpoint of the portfolio is a good place for pieces that may be a little different—perhaps more expressive and imaginative.

4. **Series.** Working on multiple pieces that go together as a series is a great way to encourage yourself to develop concepts fully. A series can be two or more pieces that have any common trait or set of traits. An example of a series concept is one with common subject matter or inspiration such as a self-portrait series. Another series may all use similar media like a series of photographs, collages, or printmaking. Yet another way to make pieces relate as a series is to select the same format or size and orientation; for example, making a series of images that are all 9″ × 12″ vertical. This is another great midpoint inclusion for your portfolio.

5. **Sketches (show personal process).** When submitting original work, sketches are usually grouped together in a book or folder. However, if you decide to submit slides or a digital portfolio, you will need to document sketches individually. You should consider ordering the images so that the sketches are grouped together, probably toward the end of the body of work, rather than placing the sketches throughout the body, which can be confusing to the viewer. You will want to limit the number of images of sketches that you submit to about five. To select slide-worthy sketches, simply go through your sketchbooks and see what appeals to you. Consider selecting pieces that show your art-making process (thumbnails and compositional sketches), technical proficiency (a good pen and ink sketch or small rendering), and any other areas that may not be fully represented through your other portfolio pieces.

6. **The finale.** Save one or two of your best pieces for last. You want the viewer to end with a strong, lasting, positive impression of your work.

(Abridged from "Preparing Your Portfolio for Review" by Brooke Hunter-Lombardi from Colombia College of Art & Design Website.
Copyright ©2006. Reprinted by permission of Brooke Hunter-Lombardi. Retrieved May 1, 2007: http://k-12.ccad.edu/article_a01.htm)

3.3.2 Traditional Portfolios for Digital Artists

Digital artists, regardless of the medium, should also create a traditional portfolio. Having a traditional portfolio will allow you to present your work at a meeting and spread a body of work out for viewing. If you are a Web designer, print out screen shots, mount them in your portfolio, and write a description about the site. It is also a good idea to include a description of the technology that is used in the website. For example, if you use any server side technology such as php, asp, or SQL, provide a description of the added functionality to the website. You should also list the use of CSS, Java Script, Flash, or integrated media players.

To improve print quality when designing websites, keep copies of the high resolution images and use them for printing. This will make a better presentation in your portfolio and will be worth the extra effort. Additionally, print your digital images on a high quality photo paper using the highest quality printer you have access to. It may also make sense to send out your images to a professional printer and have professional quality images printed.

3.3.3 Slide Portfolio

Many employers, art galleries, and art schools will require you to submit slide portfolios. This is especially true for traditional art mediums such as painting, printmaking, 3D work, and photography. Make sure to group complementary pieces together when organizing your slides. Submit your slides in a plastic or vinyl 8.5″ × 11″ pocketed protective slide sheet. Include Fifteen to Twenty slides in your presentation. You are better off having fewer slides of strong examples than just filling your slide page with mediocre work. Each slide should be labeled with your name, the title of the work, and a number. The numbers should correspond with a separate information page listing all of your slides. The information page should include the following information:

1. Your complete contact information.
2. Title of the work with its corresponding slide number.
3. Technical information about the piece including the size, medium, technique used to create the piece, and the date of completion.
4. If the work was created for a client or a class, list the client name and use or the class assignment.

A guide to shooting slides for your portfolio

Some basic photography tips
1. Shoot outdoors! The sun is the best source of light for shooting your work.
2. Gather your work together before you begin shooting.
3. Photograph the work in order of size, the largest first.
4. Emphasize your work, not, for example, the person wearing the necklace you designed. Try zooming in close.

5. Watch for "little" things—bugs crawling across a sculpture and so forth.

6. Outdoors in bright sunlight, use the same shutter speed as your film's ASA number, with the aperture set at f/16.

7. Shoot at f/11 and f/22 also, to make certain of a good exposure. (ASA 100 film works with a 1/100 or 1/125 of a second shutter speed.)

8. Artwork should be as large as possible in your view finder. Shoot as close as possible. Your work is what is important, and not mats and frames.

9. Any visible background should be neutral, even if it's as simple as an ironed sheet hung to cover the siding of your house where the work will be photographed.

10. Detail shots may be included to explain especially sensitive or informative areas. A simple "window" of paper will allow the area to be photographed clearly and closely.

11. Focus should be sharp, with three-dimensional work being totally within the depth of field.

12. Three-dimensional work should be carefully positioned for the most descriptive point of view, and lighting should enhance the volumes.

13. Consider a range of work that best shows your skills: "most recent" is not always "best." Check your sketch books, too; there are frequently little treasures hidden there.

(Adapted from: *Undergraduate Portfolio Guidelines: A Guide to Shooting Slides for Your Portfolio.* Rochester Institute of Technology: College of Imaging Arts & Sciences, Rochester, NY. http://admissions.rit.edu/pdf/Slide%20Portfolio%20Guide.pdf. Used with permission.)

The equipment
1. Manually adjustable 35mm camera (automatic cameras aren't as effective for shooting certain kinds of work)

2. Lens with macro focus (so you can focus on very close objects and details)

3. Film (daylight type such as Kodak Ektachrome 100 Daylight)

4. Light (you'll be using the sun)

5. Tripod

6. Cable release

7. Backdrop material (black velvet, seamless paper, or solid-color wall)

8. Table, easel, or plywood propped on chair (to hold work)
9. Masking tape (to hold work, remove dust from background), clamps, straight pins, push pins
10. Assistant, if possible

A word about "depth of field," which is the area of acceptable sharp focus: Your shot's depth of field should include all of the artwork; it should not include the backdrop or surrounding areas.

High "F-stop" numbers (f/16, f/22, f/32) bring more of the field into focus.

Three-dimensional artwork usually needs these higher "F-stops."

Two-dimensional work (Figure 3–2)
A. Sun: directly overhead, behind the camera (high noon).
B. Camera: positioned at the same angle, or parallel, to work.
C. Dark background: blue, grey, black.
D. Plywood, large drawing board, or cardboard.
E. Chair, adjustable drawing table, or easel.

Three-dimensional work (Figure 3–3)
A. Sun: light stronger on one side of the object (at least two hours before sunset or after sunrise).
B. Pure white reflector (large illustration board) close to object but not in picture.
C. Simple, plain surface on which to place work.
D. Dark background, out of focus.

3.4 CREATING YOUR DEMO REEL

Creating your demo reel can be very challenging and time consuming, but it is a necessity. One of the biggest mistakes people make is trying to cram everything they ever created into the reel. Remember that your demo reel is a sample of your best work, not your complete library. Employers may have fifty to one hundred reels to view and will not give you the courtesy of watching your whole reel. In fact, if they are not blown away in the first thirty seconds, your reel will end up in the trash. You need to grab the viewer right from the beginning. Put your best work first.

Remember, you are marketing yourself. Think about how movies are marketed. In a thirty- or sixty-second TV movie promo, you are given just enough of the storyline to get you interested in spending your hard-earned money on a movie ticket. A good movie trailer does not just tell

FIGURE 3-2 Two-dimensional work

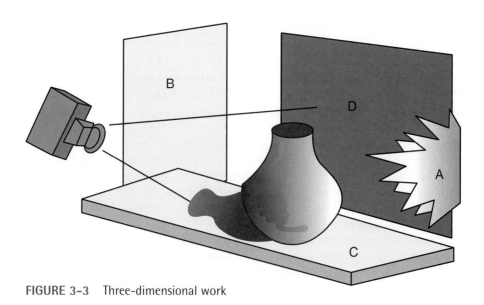

FIGURE 3-3 Three-dimensional work

you a little bit about the story; it makes you so excited about the movie that you say, "I have to see this movie!" Your goal is to get the employer to say, "I have to hire this person!"

Each studio you apply to may have very specific guidelines for submitting your demo reel. Make sure to check with the studio and ask for their guidelines.

3.4.1 Demo Reel Guidelines

- **Planning.** Do not just start editing your demo reel together. You need a plan!
  - **Review your work.** Make a list of your best work and what you did to create it. List out the techniques and software used in creating the animation.
  - **Create a storyboard.** Use the same creative process for creating a short film to create your demo reel.
- **Content.** Choose your best work only.
  - **Film and video.**
  - **Animation.** Pay attention to the lighting, texturing, and shot composition. You may use group projects, but make sure you state what you contributed to the project. You do not need to show the entire work. Showing the best twenty seconds of a one minute sequence is usually sufficient to demonstrate what you accomplished in it. Another option is to show the creative process. Perhaps you want to show the evolution from a storyboard, to a model, and finally a fully rendered version. Consider what your strongest skills are and focus on that. For example, if you consider yourself a strong modeler, set up your model with a 360-degree camera slowly rotating around it. Show the model as a wire frame, then in grayscale; next add textures and finally lighting. Dissolve from one stage of production to the next. If your model is a character and has been rigged, you may want to show a walking sequence and have the character walk off camera.
  - **Music.** When music is needed for your reel, choose it carefully. The music you choose can really help your demo reel or really hurt it. When choosing music, think of how it works in the movies. Many students make the mistake of just picking one of their favorite songs without considering how the music will work with their content. Guidelines to follow include (These are

guidelines and not rules. Use your best judgment based upon your content.):

- Use music with a quick tempo to keep your demo reel moving and engaging.

- Remember that instrumental music often works best.

- Explore the use of original music. Loop-based music composition programs such as Sony Acid, Fruity Loops, and Garage Band make it easy to compose an original soundtrack. Additionally, there are no copyright issues when composing with these programs. The source files are usually considered royalty-free.

- Edit to the beat of your music. This will help with the flow and speak highly to your attention to detail.

- When using copyrighted music, contact the publisher and request permission. It is doubtful that the owner would ever know that you used the music and, since you are not profiting off it, probably would not care; regardless, it is not a bad idea to send off an e-mail or make a phone call requesting the proper permissions. After all, would you want somebody using your original artwork without requesting your permission?

- **Time.** Demo reels should be between one and two minutes. Many students make the mistake of trying to show off everything they ever created. Your demo reel is a commercial for you; it is not a film festival. Companies that are reviewing demo reels may have hundreds of submissions to review. They do not have time to watch a demo reel that is more than Two minutes. If you have an entire animated short that you want to include on your reel, you can add it at the end of your VHS. If you are creating a DVD demo reel, create a separate section within your main menu for full length content.

- **Contact information.** Include your contact information at the end of the demo reel, on the DVD or VHS itself, and on the case. Make sure people know how to contact you if they like your work.

Do not's!

- Do not use tutorials on your demo reel. The viewer will recognize it as a tutorial and will not consider you for the position. Keep your work original.

- Do not use somebody else's work!

- Do not exceed two minutes on your demo reel.

- Do not show a spaceship flying through a tunnel. Unless it is your most outstanding piece, this is the most unoriginal animation you can place on your demo reel. Everybody has done it!

REVIEW QUESTIONS/ACTIVITIES

Write an artist's statement for a classmate

- Fill out the Artist's Statement Worksheet.
- Give a student in the class a single piece of art or a series of your creative work along with your Artist's Statement Worksheet and ask the student to draft an artist's statement for you.
- Review the statements with the class and evaluate.

Portfolio presentation

- Pretend you are presenting your portfolio to a freelance client.
- Present your portfolio to the class.
- After presenting your portfolio, discuss the creative process of the content within your portfolio.
- Have the class ask you questions about your work.

CHAPTER 4

The Job Search

OUTLINE

OBJECTIVES

- Learn how to start a job search
- Locate job resources
- Research the company

INTRODUCTION

One of the hardest parts of starting your career is locating strong job leads. This chapter is designed to give job seekers the skills to track down strong job leads and start the application process. Job searching sources including print, Web, and networking will be explored in an effort to broaden your leads.

4.1 ORGANIZATION

Starting a job search without proper organization can be an overwhelming task. With a little work, you can stay organized and land the perfect job. One method for organizing your job search is to start a binder for your job leads. Use the worksheet in Figure 4.1 to start your job search. Create a worksheet for each job lead and place it in the binder. It is also a good idea to copy or print out the job lead advertisement and attach it to the worksheet.

4.2 COMPANY RESEARCH

Finding the right job is more than getting a job offer. You need to find a place of employment that is also equally a fit for you. The corporate culture, types of projects you will be working on, and your supervisor are all things to consider when applying and accepting a job offer. It takes more than a job interview to know if you will be happy at a place of employment. You will need to conduct your own research about the company.

The first place to start is the company's website. Most companies today have extensive websites that highlight information such as the type of business, list of clients, profiles of executives, recent projects, products produced, corporate history, press releases, and a listing of current positions available at the company. This information will give you a great sense of who the company is and what the company does. It may also give you great insight into the corporate culture. Is the website flashy and hip or traditional and conservative? What type of clients are they targeting?

4.2.1 Researching Publicly Traded Companies

There are many sources for conducting research about a company; especially if it is a publicly traded company (one that is traded on a stock exchange such as the NASDAQ or New York Stock Exchange). This means that anybody can buy or sell shares of this company. For as little as a few dollars, you too can purchase a small piece of the company.

JOB LEAD WORKSEET

Company Contact:

Name of Company: _____

Address: _____

_____

Phone Number: _____ Fax: _____

Website: _____ E-mail _____

Job Lead Source: _____

Job Description: _____

_____

_____

_____

_____

Required Qualification: _____

_____

_____

_____

_____

Applying for the Position Directions: _____

_____

List How Your Background Matches the Job Requirements: _____

_____

_____

_____

_____

Date Resume and Cover Letter Sent: _____

Person Who You Sent Information to: _____

Follow-Up Phone Call   **Date:**_____

(*Call one week later to confirm they received your resume*)

Interview Date: _____ **Interview Time:** _____

List All Names of People You Interviewed with:

Name	Title:	Thank-You Note Sent (check):	Comments:

Notes from Interview: _____

_____

_____

_____

Interview Self-Analysis: *Create a list of what you did well and areas that need improvement during the interview.*

Strong Points:	Areas Needing Improvement:
Made strong impression with portfolio.	*Make more eye contact when answering questions.*

Follow-Up Phone Call (*Call two weeks after interview to check application status*):

Date: _____ Person Contacted: _____

Second Interview Date: _____ **Interview Time:** _____

List All Names of people You Interviewed with:

Name	Title:	Thank-You Note Sent (check):	Comments:

Notes from Interview: _____

_____

_____

_____

Interview Self-Analysis: *Create a list of what you did well and areas that need improvement during the interview.*

Strong Points:	Areas Needing Improvement:

Follow-Up Phone Call (*Call two weeks after interview to check application status*):

Date: _____ **Person Contacted:** _____

FIGURE 4–1   Job lead worksheet

Publicly traded companies are required to file both quarterly and annual reports. These reports highlight a company's financial health and project their outlook for the short-and-long term future. Reviewing this report will give you great insight into the company's health and growth. Perhaps the company is shrinking and laying off hundreds of workers. If this is the case, you might want to look for a job someplace else. Perhaps the company is starting a new division. This could represent a great opportunity to get involved in a new venture on the ground floor of a launch. Although riskier, the upside and the ability to get promoted in this type of situation might make this type of opportunity more appealing.

In addition to annual reports, there are many other research sources for publicly traded companies. Brokerage houses and financial research companies such as *Standard and Poors* and *Value Line* conduct research and publish reports about publicly traded companies. These reports usually require either a subscription to a service or can often be

> Many financial research companies will provide you with a free
> trial period to try out their services. Use the free trial periods to
> conduct extensive research about a company before going on the
> interview.

found in financial magazines. Additionally, if you have a brokerage
account, most brokerage companies include free market research as a
benefit to having an account. Furthermore, most libraries, including
college libraries, have access to these publications that you can view for
free. Table 4.1 shows a listing of sources.

4.2.2 Check Their Profile

Most companies today use Internet classified services such as Monster,
Hotjobs, and Career Builder to advertise their job openings. Many of
the hiring companies list a profile of their company at these sites. The
brief company profile listed can help you find your next source for
research. The profile will highlight the business type as well as the size
of the company and the industry.

4.2.3 The Inside Scoop

To find out if a company is ethical and a place where you want to work,
you will have to do some creative research. One way to get information
about a company's business practices is to check with the Council of
Better Business Bureaus (BBB). The BBB is a consumer's rights organization that works with consumers and businesses to resolve consumer complaints. The BBB publishes the number of complaints
against a company, the type of complaint, and whether the complaint
has been resolved. The service is free and you can search their databases at *www.bbb.org*. Although this site does not provide employee
feedback, it does give you a good idea of the type of operation the
company runs.

Another tactic that may help you find out information about an
employer is to Google them. Try typing the company's name in a search
engine and see what comes up. You should be able to find recent
articles, press releases, customers who listed the company on their own
websites, and possibly blogs about the company. Be cautious with the information you find on the Web. However, is it a reputable source? It
might just be a blog by a disgruntled employee. However, if you see an
extensive amount of negative information about a company from multiple
sources, it might raise a red flag for you.

If you know somebody who works at a company, ask that person how
he or she likes it. Your personal network is certainly going to be one of
your strongest resources in finding a job, specifically an employee-friendly

TABLE 4-1 List of Several Financial Research Sources

Website/Company	Fee	About the Publication
Yahoo Finance *http://finance.yahoo.com/*	Free	Free research, company profiles, news archives, industry news, comparisons, and rankings. Investing articles, education, and discussion boards for each stock. **This is a great place to start your research of a company.**
Morningstar *www.morningstar.com*	Free membership with registration. Free Fourteen day trial of premium membership.	Advanced research and rankings of companies and various funds. Company discussion boards, article archive, free investing classes, stock analyst reports on 1,800 stocks.
The Motley Fool *www.fool.com*	Free membership with registration. Free Thirty day trial of Motley Fool Stock Advisor and other premium services.	Articles, research, stock ratings, financial advice, message boards, retirement planning, financial education.
Wall Street Journal Online *www.wsj.com*	Free trial and special student rates.	Current financial news and news archives. Advanced research tools, e-mail alerts, and portfolio tracking.
Fidelity *www.fidelity.com*	Free Thirty day trial	Over 4,500 analyst ratings and reports, brokerage services, mutual funds, and advanced research.
Value Line *www.valueline.com*	Pay service. Available at your library for free.	Independent research of over 8,000 stocks and other investment research.
Google Finance *http://finance.google.com/*	Free	Free research, company profiles, news archives, discussion boards, industry news, comparisons, and rankings. Investing articles and education.

TABLE 4-1 (Continued)

Website/Company	Fee	About the Publication
MSN Money *http://moneycentral* *.msn.com/*	Free	Free research, company profiles, news archives, discussion boards, industry news, comparisons, and rankings. Investing articles and education.
CNN Money *http://money.cnn.com/*	Free	Internet site for Fortune, Money, Business 2.0, and Fortune Small Business. Free research, company profiles, news archives, industry news, comparisons, and rankings. Investing articles and education.

job. If you do not know anybody who works at the company, ask one of your professors, employment coordinators and internship coordinators, at your school. If the potential job is in your area, there is a good chance that one of these people has worked with the company. Even after you have graduated, these sources at your alma mater continue to be a great resource for you. Take advantage of them.

4.2.4 Industry Magazines and Websites

Most industries have publications that are specific to their field, especially in the media and design fields. Magazines and Web-based publications concentrate on technology, designing skills, and industry news. Often, these publications will have feature articles on companies and professionals in the industry. These publications can give you great insight into industry trends and which companies are up and coming. Additionally, mentioning that you read about the company in a specific publication will impress the interviewer and show that you stay current on industry trends.

In addition to important industry news, most industry publications have a classified section. Employers use industry-specific classified sections to target the exact people they are trying to recruit. You may find job leads in these industry-specific magazines that are not advertised in larger publications and websites such as Monster.com and Hotjobs.com.

4.3 FINDING JOB LEADS

Obviously finding strong job leads is the key to landing a job. There are many sources for job leads including networking, print, the Web, employment agencies, government agencies, head-hunters, and your school's career services department. When searching for a job, it is important to use a number of sources; do not just search the Web.

4.3.1 Networking

Networking, meeting people in the industry, is one of the best ways to land a job. Networking is also essential for success in any industry. So the question is how does a person entering a new industry start to network? You can use many methods to start and build your network. Some examples include:

- **Internships.** One of the best ways to meet industry professionals and get your foot in the door is to work as an intern at a company in your field. This will serve several purposes:

  - **Vital industry experience.** The classroom is a vital part of your education and will teach you a lot in terms of theory, best practices, and technique; however, one of the most difficult lessons to teach in a classroom is how to work within the industry, work with clients, and experience working on a commercial project. An internship is the part of your education that introduces you to the professional world, lets you experience a real deadline, and allows you to work with paying customers.

  - **Meet industry professionals.** Since you are working in a commercial facility, each person you meet is someone to add to your network. Many interns do not take their internships seriously. This is a mistake. The impression you make with the people within that company and their clients is the beginning of your professional reputation. Most industries are small and your reputation as a hard-working and talented person will help you land a job.

  - **Build your portfolio.** Nothing will help you grow your portfolio better than professional work. School projects are important and will show diversity, but including commercial work from paying clients will establish you as a professional.

  - **Land a job offer.** Your job search may be over before you ever graduate from school. Most companies will offer a talented, hard-working intern an entry-level position before advertising the job and interviewing strangers. Companies offer internships because it gives them extra help around the office and provides the employer with a free test drive of a potential employee. Even if the company that you are interning at does not have an opening, they may know another company in the industry that is hiring. All it may

STUDENT DISCOUNTED MEMBERSHIP

Most industry organizations offer discounts to students to join their organization. Make sure you take advantage of these discounted rates and these organizations while you are still a student.

take for you to land a job is a phone call from your internship supervisor to another employer saying, "You should hire this kid! (S)He is one of the most talented and reliable interns we have ever had!"

- **Industry organizations.** Joining industry organizations such as the Graphic Artist Guild (GAG), the National Association of Television Program Executives (NATPE), and the National Association of Broadcasters (NAB) are vital to establishing yourself as a professional and for networking within an industry. Most organizations have regular meetings in your area and many host annual conventions. These meetings and conventions are the perfect place to network, since everybody in attendance is an industry professional. Make sure you have your resume and a business card to hand out when you meet new industry people. It is also highly recommended that you have copies of your digital portfolio to hand out with your resume. Another option is to have a website portfolio listed on your resume. (See Chapter 1 for a list of industry organizations.)

- **Job fairs.** Job fairs are a great place to network. Hiring companies attend job fairs for one reason: to recruit employees. Job fairs may be organized by your school or hosted at a local convention center. When attending job fairs, dress your best and bring your business card, a stack of your resumes, and your portfolio. It is best to have several copies of your digital portfolio with you to leave with potential employers. The job fair is all about first impressions.

  - **Sell yourself.** You need to be able to sell yourself in a short time period to get an interview. Be prepared to discuss your skills and experience. Keep a list of all your credits, as well as the skills and software you are trained in. Review your notes throughout the day to keep your strong points fresh in your mind.

  - **Collect business cards.** One advantage of attending job fairs versus sending your resume to a company is meeting a recruiter from that company. Make sure to ask for business cards from everybody you meet. After meeting several companies, you will not necessarily remember everything you told each

CONVENTIONS

Many industry organizations such as the National Association of Television Program Executives (NATPE), the National Association of Broadcasters (NAB), and the Audio Engineering Society (AES) have annual conventions in fun cities such as New York, Los Angeles, Miami, and Las Vegas. At the conventions, vendors and industry professionals set up booths to demonstrate the latest technologies and various services offered. In addition, there are usually workshops and seminars scheduled throughout the week of the convention demonstrating industry, techniques, discussing trends in the industry and hosting social networking dinners. Conventions are all about networking. Do not miss these opportunities.

TAX DEDUCTION TIP

Your dues to industry organizations and the costs associated with attending conventions are usually tax deductible to you. Discuss this possibility with your accountant or other tax professional.

company. Therefore, keep a note pad with you and take notes on all of the companies that you give your resume to.

- **Follow-up.** Send an e-mail or letter to the recruiter within Twenty-Four hours of meeting them, thanking the recruiter for his or her time at the job fair, expressing your interest in the company, and requesting an interview.

- **Your professors.** Your professors at school are probably involved in the industry. This is especially true in design and media fields, where most professors either work full-time within the industry and adjunct at colleges or are full-time professors who freelance on the side. Either way, they are involved with many professionals in the field and may be able to recommend you to a company. *(Obviously with these types of connections in the industry, you want to show your professors how reliable you are. A professor is not going to recommend you if you're late to class often and do not meet assignment deadlines. These are the things employers are looking for.)*

- **Volunteer your services.** Find a local charity or organization that can use your services and volunteer. Some possible ways to volunteer include designing a website for a local government official

ORGANIZATION AND PUBLICATION LINKS

To see an updated list of industry organizations and publications, visit: *www.careercrib.com.*

or office, creating marketing material for a charity fundraiser, and volunteering at a local Boys and Girls Club to teach art. Since most of these organizations are vital to your community, word of your great work will spread fast and you may meet both potential freelance clients and employers. *Volunteering also looks great on a resume!*

4.3.2 Print Classified Advertisements

Your local newspaper is certainly a first place to look for local jobs. In terms of newspaper advertisements, most papers are regional. Therefore, you need to find papers that target your geographical area. However, there are several other print sources to consider. Trade newspapers and trade magazines have classified sections in the back of the publications. Any employment opportunities listed will probably be targeted to your industry. Do not disregard print classifieds; it might have the job lead you are looking for.

When looking for a job in the classifieds, make sure you are searching under several headings. For example, if you are looking for a job in Graphic Design, you need to expand your search beyond the term Graphic Designer. A few examples of job title categories to search include: advertising, marketing, printing, multimedia, Web Designer, Animator, Design, and prepress. It is important to expand your job search beyond the main title of the position you are looking for. The same skill set you possess may qualify you for several positions.

4.3.3 Internet-Based Job Search

The Internet certainly makes searching for a job convenient. Internet job sources include general employment websites such as Monster.com and Hotjob.com, industry-specific websites such as GAG.org and Career-Crib.com, and company-specific websites such as Disney.com. Most large companies host their own searchable job listings. There are so many potential sources for jobs, it can often seem overwhelming. The key is focusing your job search to your needs and finding the best sources that will work for you.

How do you find a strong job lead? When searching large sites, the keywords you use will dictate the job leads that return from your search. The obvious keywords most people use are the title of the job they are seeking. However, a successful job search requires a little creativity. For example, in searching for a job as a Graphic Designer, in addition to searching the keyword "Graphic Designer," try searching some of the skills, related to being a Graphic Designer. Search software titles, related skills, and duties. A Graphic Designer may use search terms such as: "Web Designer," "Photoshop," "Illustrator," "Dreamweaver," "Artist," "Preflighting," "Multimedia," and so on.

Job search engines do not just search the title of the job advertisement. The search engines will search the entire text of the job listing. This will enable you to search for job-specific items such as software, job requirements, and specific duties. A few tips for optimizing your job search include:

1. Search by geographic area.

2. Use **Boolean Operators** to help narrow your search. For example, instead of searching for the term "Web Designer," use Boolean Operators such as "and," "or," and "not." A Boolean will combine terms or exclude them based upon which Boolean operation you choose. For example, when searching for a video editing job that uses Final Cut Pro, you may search, "Video Editor and Final Cut Pro." This Boolean-based search will help narrow down editing jobs that require knowledge of Final Cut Pro.

3. Place your keyword search in quotes to find a specific string of words. When you type in words without quotes, most search engines break up the sentence into individual words and search for each word's occurrence. By placing the sentence in quotes, the search engine will search for the entire string of words as listed in the quotes.

4. To expand a search, try a **wild card search**. A wild card search will allow for variations of your key terms. Using an asterisk ("*"), the search engine will replace the asterisk with any terms connected to the non-wild card term. For example, if you were looking for a job working in video production within a ten mile radius of your zip code, a search of "Video Editor" may return eight job leads. However, if you search with a wild card such as "Video*," your job lead return may give you back twenty leads. In addition to the eight job leads of Video Editors, you would also get terms such as Video Producer, Video Assistant, and any other term that includes the word "Video" in it.

Table 4.2 is a list of job searching websites.

TABLE 4–2 Web Job Sources

Website	Specialty and Description	Post a Resume	Build a Resume	Create a Search Agent	Other Resources
www.monster.com	General employment website	Yes	Yes	Yes	Loaded with extras including: interview center, salary center, self-assessment tools, cover letter tips, and a wealth of other resources.
www.hotjobs.com	General employment website	Yes	Yes	Yes	Loaded with extras including: interview center, salary center, self-assessment tools, cover letter tips, and a wealth of other resources.
www.careerbuilder.com	General employment website	Yes	Yes	Yes	Loaded with extras including: interview center, salary center, self-assessment tools, cover letter tips, and a wealth of other resources.
www.gag.org/ jobline/Graphic Artist Guild	Weekly newsletter	No	No	No	Members only newsletter. You must be a member and sign up for the newsletter.
www.careercrib.com	Design and media career advice portal	Yes	Yes	Yes	Resume builder with templates, bulletin board, career advice, cover letter samples, portfolio samples.
www.mandy.com	International film and TV production resources	No	No	No	Film and TV services database, casting center, vendors, notice board, film market.

(Continued)

TABLE 4-2 (Continued)

Website	Specialty and Description	Post a Resume	Build a Resume	Create a Search Agent	Other Resources
www3Dartist.com	Resources for 3D artist	No	No	No	Online magazine, classified ads, 3D artist directory, articles on specific software.
www.raph.com	Resources for 3D artist	Yes	Yes	Yes	Art gallery, interviews, tutorials, forums, newsletter.
www.3dcafe.com	Resources for 3D artist	No	No	No	Art gallery, tutorials, list of schools, forums, classified.
www.craigslist.com	Bulletin board for everything	No	No	No	Search by area for full-time, part-time, and freelance work.
www.awn.com Animation World Network	Resources for 2D and 3D artist	Yes	Yes	No	News, forums, online magazine, career coach, school database, many other resources.
www.cgsociety.org Society of Digital Artists	Resources for 3D artist	No	No	No	Forum with job board, workshops, store, gallery, newsletter.
www.dice.com	Tech job board	Yes	Yes	Yes	Specializes in technology jobs.
www.collegegrad. com	Entry-level job resources	Yes	Yes	Yes	Great resources for new college graduates.
www.careerjournal. com Wall Street Journal's career site	General employment website	Yes	Yes	Yes	Loaded with extras including: interview center, salary center, self assessment tools, cover letter tips and a wealth of other resources.

Website	Specialty and Description	Post a Resume	Build a Resume	Create a Search Agent	Other Resources
www.coroflot.com	Careers for creative people	Yes	Yes	No	Create an online portfolio, job search, industry advice.
www.artsopport unities.org	Arts and media employment	No	No	No	Free job board
www.computerjobs. com	IT and computer-related jobs	Yes	Yes	Yes	Job board, section for creative computer jobs, additional resources links
www.creativehotlist. com	Careers for Creative people	Yes	No	No	Create an online portfolio, promote your business.
www.gignews.com	Game industry resources	No	No	No	Job board, online magazine, career advise
www.creativeplanet. com	Film and television resources	No	No	No	Forums, job board, industry news.
www.allfreelance work.com	Freelancer resources	No	No	No	Post your portfolio, job board, forums.
www.allfreelance. com/	Freelancer resources	No	No	No	Post your portfolio, job board, forums.
www.freeagent.com	Freelancer resources	Yes	Yes	Yes	List your skills—employers can search by skills.
www.gamasutra .com	Gaming and multimedia resources	Yes	No	No	News, job board, post resume, education, product reviews.
www.Gamejobs. com	Gaming and multimedia resources	Yes	Yes	Yes	Build and post a resume, create a search agent, search database.
www.games-match.com	Gaming and interactive media jobs	Yes	Yes	No	Job board, resume builder, forums.

(Continued)

TABLE 4-2   (Continued)

Website	Specialty and Description	Post a Resume	Build a Resume	Create a Search Agent	Other Resources
www.GetThat Gig.com	General employment website	Yes	Yes	No	Interviews and tips from professionals.
www.guru.com	Freelancer website	Yes	Yes	No	Resource for posting and finding freelancers and specialists.
www.dice.com	Technology jobs	Yes	Yes	Yes	Resume writing tips, advanced search features.
www.portfolios.com	View and post portfolios	No	No	No	Job board, post and view portfolios, fee based system (sixty-day free trial).
www.recruiters online.com	Headhunter source	Yes	No	No	Database of recruiters by specialty.
www.screenmag.tv	Film and TV online magazine	No	No	No	Resources for film and television.
www.creativeheads. net	Job board of siggraph	Yes	No	No	Create online profile, search by industry.
www.fxguide.com	FX For film, TV, and animation	Yes	No	No	Freelancer listing, bulletin board, tutorials, news.
www.bluegeckonet work.com	Web development network	Yes	No	No	Job board, forums, directory, bid on freelance jobs.
www.contracted work.com	Media and design freelance network	Yes	No	No	Bid on freelance jobs, fee-based listing service.
www.jobsearchsite. com	General employment website	Yes	No	Yes	Free newsletter, all industry database of jobs, career resources.

Website	Specialty and Description	Post a Resume	Build a Resume	Create a Search Agent	Other Resources
www.graphicartist designer.com	Design and media careers	Yes	No	Yes	Free online portfolio, career resources.

(An updated list is located at: *http://www.careercrib.com/search_source.html*)

4.3.4 Headhunters and Employment Agencies

Headhunters (recruiters) actively recruit employees on behalf of an employer seeking to fill an important vacancy. Often these positions are harder to fill and are not entry-level positions. If you have a reputation in the industry, a headhunter may approach you. You may also submit your resume to a headhunter in response to a job search an employer is trying to fill. In some cases, a headhunter will represent an employee seeking a job and shop you to potential employers. This can be a very effective way to find a position if the headhunter has a strong reputation in the industry for placing talented employees. Usually the hiring employer pays the headhunter, not the job seeker.

Employment agencies are employment services that assist job seekers in finding employment. Unlike a headhunter, employment agencies do not actively recruit. Job seekers need to actively seek out the employment agency's assistance. Some employment agencies will charge a fee to the job seeker, so ask up front and try to avoid these services. There are plenty of agencies that will charge the fee to the employer.

Temporary employment agencies are similar to regular employment agencies except their job placements fill temporary vacancies. Often, companies will need a temporary employee to fill a vacancy while a current employee is away on vacation, maternity leave or family leave. They simply fill a temporary need for extra staffing. Although most graduates are seeking permanent full-time positions, accepting temporary employment will help you gain experience, make you money immediately, and possibly lead to a full-time job offer. If you make a strong impression as a temporary employee, the company will remember you when a permanent position becomes available.

U.S. DEPARTMENT OF LABOR

www.dol.gov

The U.S. Department of Labor is the government agency in charge of developing a stronger workforce and is in charge of enforcing federal labor laws. The DOL website also has a list of numerous links to various related government agencies, labor laws, employment websites, and listings for your state's local DOL website. Your local DOL office and website, will have free job postings and will also allow you to post your resume for employers to search. Since the service is free to both employers and job seekers, it is a great place to start your job search.

REVIEW QUESTIONS/ACTIVITIES

Group job search:

- See which group can find the most relevant jobs for students to apply for.
- Divide the class into groups of three to five students.
- Divide a list of print publications and employment websites among the different groups.
- Assign a different member from each group to a specific source to search for jobs (print classifieds, specific websites, etc.).
- After fifteen minutes of searching, share with the class the different job leads your group found.

Writing an Effective Cover Letter

OUTLINE

OBJECTIVES

- Learn how to draft an effective cover letter
- Create a cover letter that addresses the company's needs
- Create a cover letter presentation

INTRODUCTION

So you have found a company that you want to work for. Now how do you get their attention? If the company likes your resume they will read your cover letter. Since we have already covered how to write a strong resume, now we will focus on drafting a cover letter that will get you a job interview.

Your cover letter provides the chance to tell an employer exactly why they should hire you. When drafting your cover letter, consider what you would tell this company if you had their attention for five minutes and getting the job depends on it, because it does. The bottom line is, if your cover letter does not address their needs, you are probably not going to get an interview.

5.1 EFFECTIVE COVER LETTER WRITING

1. **Appearance.** Keep the appearance of your cover letter clean and concise. Make sure you use the same type of high quality paper for your cover letter and resume. Keep the formatting consistent and break important sections into separate paragraphs. Use a simple font that is easy to read with a type size of at least ten points, but no larger than twelve points. *Make sure to include your contact information as a header on top of the document. Include your name, address, phone number, and e-mail.* Although this information is on your resume, the pages may get separated.

2. **The addressee.** It is always a good idea to target your resume to the person who will be reading it. Writing "To Whom It May Concern" or "To the Human Resource Manager" is not as effective as addressing your letter to the head of the department or resume screener directly. Call the company and ask who to address the letter to. Also, make sure to get the correct spelling and title of the individual. The only exception to this rule is if the job listing specifically directs you to a specific department and addressee or specifies, "no phone calls."

3. **The opening.** Make sure to state the title or position you are applying for and how you heard of the job in the opening of the cover letter.

4. **Keep it simple and direct.** Keep your wording concise and to the point. State your qualities and how they will benefit the employer. Directly address their job requirements listed in the job description. You may bullet your top three to five qualities as an itemized list. This helps draw attention to the top qualities that you want the employer to focus on.

Do not waste cover letter space with useless fluff. The employer may be reading letters and resumes from more than 100 applicants and they want to know how you are going to help them. Keep your letter to less than a page and make sure you sign it on the bottom.

5. **Focus on the company.** Make sure to focus your cover letter on the company's needs. When speaking of your qualities and assets, express them as a means of satisfying their requirements for the available position. The employer is interested in what you are going to do for them. They are not interested in improving your resume. Researching the company will give you insight to the type of clients they work with. This will help you focus your cover letter. Do not start off every sentence with "I" or "my."

6. **Grammar and spelling.** *Employers are looking for effective communicators.* Your cover letter is the first piece of communication they are going to read from you. If your letter is filled with spelling and grammar mistakes, they will probably not call you despite your qualifications. Use your word processor's spelling and grammar checker. Then read your letter out loud to yourself to make sure the phrasing reads correctly. Finally, ask or hire someone professional to proofread your letter.

7. **Honesty.** Do not lie or exaggerate in your letter. If you misrepresent yourself, the employer will figure it out during the interview. Overstating your qualifications may prohibit you from ever being considered for another position at that company.

5.2 DIFFERENT TYPES OF COVER LETTERS

1. **Advertisement response letter.** This letter is in response to a job advertisement or bulletin. An advertisement response letter gives you an opportunity to directly respond to a specific set of criteria that the employer is looking for. The employer will list the qualifications including skill level, education, and work experience that they are seeking. Use your cover letter to address each point in their advertisement. Point out how your training and background addresses their point-by-point needs.

In the opening paragraph of your letter, make sure you state what position you are applying for and where you learned of the available position. For example, "I am sending this letter and enclosed resume as an application for the position of Video Editing Assistant as posted at Monster.com."

TIP

Cold letters can be sent to companies that you may have had contact with in the past. Contacts that you have met through networking often make great people to send a cold letter to. Try sending a letter to a former guest speaker from your school or a seminar you attended and mention something particular the speaker spoke about. You can also mention how their speech left an impression on you.

---

2. **Referral letter.** One of the most effective ways to obtain a job is through networking. Referrals from existing employees or companies that have a relationship with the employer will give you an advantage over other applicants. A recommendation from a respected employee gives credibility to your application for employment. Make sure you mention the person referring you in your cover letter. For example, "Jane Smith recommended that I contact you in reference to current openings within your Design Department."

3. **Cold letter.** A cold letter is a general letter of inquiry and is not in response to a specific vacancy notice. Often people who have an interest in working for a specific company will send a general letter expressing their interest in working for that company. This type of letter can be effective if written well and accompanied by a strong resume. In your cover letter express your interest for the department and (or) position you would be interested in. Then proceed to highlight your ability to enhance their business. For example,

"I am writing to inquire about any current or future employment opportunities in your Web Design Department."

or

"As a recent graduate from New York University, I am in search of an entry-level position in your Advertising Department."

Then proceed to highlight your qualifications.

5.3 RESEARCH THE COMPANY

Before drafting your cover letter, make sure you have a strong understanding of what the company does and, more importantly, what they need. While searching for a job you should have created a job database

(Chapter 4). Use the information from your database to help you structure your letter. Understanding their needs will help you focus your letter and grab the attention of the reader.

Your letter should demonstrate the following:

1. Your understanding of the company and its clients.
2. Your ability to satisfy the company's needs.
3. Most importantly, your ability to effectively communicate.

COMMUNICATION IS KEY

Your cover letter will demonstrate your ability to be an effective communicator. Employers need to know that you can express your ideas in a cohesive presentation. Your cover letter is the employer's first sample of your ability to express yourself. If your letter has mistakes or is not coherent, you will not get the job.

5.4 DRAFTING THE LETTER AND SAMPLES

5.4.1 Advertisement Response Letter

Although this is not the most effective and efficient method for finding a job, with persistence it can result in a positive experience. Use a broad search of the internet, newspapers, and trade magazines to locate job advertisements. These postings will ask you to respond in a predefined way. Response methods may include asking you to fill out an online job application, and/or present your resume in person, via e-mail, or through traditional mail. In each case, make sure to follow the instructions as defined in the job posting. In all cases, make sure to attach a letter when possible. The worksheet in Figure 5–1 will help you draft a response cover letter.

RESPONSE LETTER WORKSHEET

Company Name: _____

Company Address: _____

_____

Contact Name or Addressee to send resume to: _____

Contact e-mail Address: _____

Contact Phone Number: _____

Position Seeking: _____

Education Requirements: _____

Number of Years of Related Experience Required: _____

List of Computer Skills Required: _____

_____

_____

List of Related Skills Required: _____

_____

_____

List All of Your Software Skills That Apply to This Job: _____

_____

_____

_____

_____

Summarize Your Related Skills and Other Personal Traits That Are Applicable to This Position:_____

_____

_____

_____

_____

_____

FIGURE 5-1   Response letter worksheet

Sample Response Cover Letters (Figures 5.2, 5.3, and 5.4)

Response Letter

This letter is in response to an entry-level Web Design position. The author highlights her experience that directly relates to the job posting requirements. She bullets key points to draw attention to the most important aspects of her experience.

Melissa Smith

211 5th Avenue · Boston, MA 02331 · (415) 555-5555 · e-mail: M_Smith@Pratt.edu

June 12, 20XX

James Washington
Website Innovators, INC.
1234 Brewster Street
Boston, MA 02335

To Mr. Washington:

I am sending this letter, enclosed resume, and CD-ROM portfolio in response to your advertisement for an entry-level Web Designer as posted at CareerCrib.com. I am well trained in the technical aspects of Web design and have a keen sense of page layout that will help contribute to your creative team immediately. My experience and skills include:

- Advanced software knowledge of Dreamweaver, Flash, Director, Cold Fusion, Imageready, Photoshop, Illustrator, and Fireworks.
- Hand coding and proficiency in HTML, XHTML, CSS, and Java Script.
- A basic understanding with some experience in ASP, PHP, MySQL, and server side scripting.
- Possess a great sense of designing skills including training in typography, color theory, and composition.

As demonstrated in my enclosed digital portfolio, my experience includes a diverse sample of Web-based projects that include Web animation designed in Flash, e-commerce design, and implementation of basic server side scripting with customized bulletin boards and creation of e-mail databases. I am capable of working as a member of a team or individually. Additionally, I am eager to learn and pick up new concepts fast with great efficiency.

I would greatly appreciate the opportunity to interview with you. I will call you next Wednesday to confirm that you received this letter and answer any questions you may have.

Sincerely,

Melissa Smith

Melissa Smith

FIGURE 5-2   Sample response cover letter

Response Letter

This letter is in response to an entry-level Game Level Designer job posting. The author is responding directly to the requirements posted in the job advertisement and is also emphasizing an understanding of the company's product.

Andrew Jones

37 West John Street · Chicago, IL 60605 · 708.555.5555 · e-mail: Andy_Jones@Careercrib.com

April 12, 20XX

Jocelyn Jennings
Retro Gaming Unlimited
1223 5th Avenue
New York, NY 10014

Dear Ms. Jocelyn Jennings:

As I plan on relocating to Manhattan upon my graduation this May, your advertisement for an Assistant Game Artist/Animator in Underground *Gaming Magazine* caught my attention. Your company's history of bringing back classic video games with a cutting edge design has created a gaming trend in which I can contribute greatly to. My passion for gaming is relentless and I have excelled at character modeling while in school.

My software skills include three years experience in 3D Studio Max, Photoshop, and The Unreal Editor. Excelling as one of the top character modelers in my graduating class, I specialize in both Low Polygon Modeling and High Polygon Pre-Rendered Graphics. Often, I have functioned as a peer tutor to other students in my program. Additionally, I am well skilled in texturing, rigging, and level design.

I am very capable of working as a team member or working individually. Additionally, I have a knack for picking up software and animation techniques fast and efficiently. Skills that may also interest you are my traditional storyboarding skills and story development writing.

I will be in New York the first week in May and will be available for an interview. Additionally, I am immediately available via phone and e-mail to discuss the position and my qualifications. I will call you early next week to answer any questions you may have.

Sincerely,

Andrew Jones

Andrew Jones

enclosure: Resume, DVD Portfolio

FIGURE 5-3   Sample response cover letter

Response Letter

This letter is a sample of a two-column format that directly addresses the job requirements in a job posting. The first column lists the company's requirements. The second column addresses each point with a specific example of the author's qualifications and experience. This letter is precise, to the point, and very effective.

Jennifer Gonzales
3244 Harold Street
Los Angeles, CA 90008
(213) 555-9214
Jennyphoto@Careercrib.com

April 15, 20xx

ABC Photographers
322 Main Street
Los Angeles, CA 90010
Attn: Mr. Dan D. Fotagafer

To Mr. Fotagafer:

I am sending this letter in response to your recent advertisement at CareerCrib.com in search of a Photographer Assistant. I will be graduating Ohio University with a BFA in Photojournalism next month and based upon your job description I am the perfect candidate for the position for the following reasons:

Job Requirements:	My Experience:
Maintain Studio, Camera Equipment, and Lighting	Served as work study lab assistant in charge of school's photo studios and handled sign out of equipment for students.
Two years Photography Experience	Worked as a freelance photography assistant for several local wedding companies. Duties included: Second camera shooting in both portrait and B&W

Job Requirements:	My Experience:
	photojournalism styles using traditional film cameras and high resolution Nikon Digital Cameras. Assisted with film development, scanning negatives, and archiving client digital files.
Software Skills: Photoshop and MS Office	Experienced Photoshop image editor with nine credits in digital image editing. Skills include Photo Retouching (image sharpening, color correction, cropping, and perspective transforming), Image Compositing, and Advanced Layering Skills. Strong knowledge of MS Word and Excel.
Customer Service Experience	As a wedding assistant I often had to work with distraught brides and inebriated guests. Balancing the needs of the photo shoot and keeping the client happy is my specialty.

In addition to my highlighted experience above, I am also fluent in Spanish and can act as a translator for any Spanish-speaking clients you may have.

I would greatly appreciate the opportunity to interview with you. I will call you next week to confirm that you received this letter and to set up an appointment to review my portfolio.

Sincerely,

Jennifer Gonzales

Jennifer Gonzales

Enclosure: Resume

FIGURE 5-4   Sample response cover letter

5.4.2 Referral Letter

Referral letters can be written in reference to a conversation with a current employee from another department, same department, or executive. You can also be referred by anybody who has contact with the company such as a vendor, professor, or any other network of people. This type of letter is like having a built-in reference with your resume. Most vacancies in companies are filled through referrals. Use the worksheet in Figure 5–5 to help you draft a referral cover letter.

INSIDER'S TIP

Many companies offer bonuses to employees who refer new candidates for employment.

REFERRAL WORKSHEET

Company Name: _____

Company Address: _____

_____

Contact Name or Addressee to Send Resume to: _____

Contact E-mail Address: _____

Contact Phone Number: _____

Name/Title/Department/Company of Person Referring You:_____

_____

Position(s) Seeking: _____

Number of Years of Related Experience Required: _____

List of Computer Skills Required: _____

_____

_____

List of Related Skills Required: _____

_____

_____

List All of Your Software Skills That Apply to This Job: _____

_____

_____

_____

_____

Summarize Your Related Skills and Other Personal Traits That Are Applicable to This Position: _____

_____

_____

_____

_____

_____

FIGURE 5-5   Referral worksheet

Sample referral cover letters

Referral Letter

This letter is a sample of a referral letter. It directly mentions the person who referred the author. It also highlights the writer's experience and how it will address the needs of the company.

John J. Designer
212 Brookville Hall
Brookville, NY 11545
516-555-3456
JDesigner@careercrib.com

April 20, 20xx

Ms. Jane Doe
Art Director
Web Sites Unlimited
1324 Broadway
New York, NY 11112

To Ms. Doe:

I was referred to you by Prof. Smith, a Professor at C.W. Post University, who informed me that your Web Design Firm is looking for new talent.

I have more than two years of Web design experience, including interning as a Web Designer at Home Bank National, a Mortgage Bank located in Manhattan. I will be receiving my BA this May from Long Island University—C.W. Post, graduating Magna Cum Laude. I am confident that my combination of design skills and solid educational experience has prepared me for making an immediate contribution to Web Sites Unlimited.

Having interned with a company that allowed me to design and maintain their website, as well as design their marketing material; I understand the level of professionalism required for contributing to the success of your business. My background and professional approach to design and usability will provide your company with a highly productive Designer who will continue your company's tradition of delivering innovative designs that your clients are looking for.

I would greatly appreciate the opportunity to show you my portfolio. Please call me at 516-555-3456 to arrange a convenient time for an interview. If I have not heard from you by May 17, I will contact your office to inquire as to a potential meeting date and time. Thank you for your time and consideration.

Sincerely,
John J. Designer
John J. Designer

enclosure: Resume

FIGURE 5-6   Sample referral cover letter

Referral Letter

This is a sample of a referral letter. It directly mentions the person who referred the author. It also directly responds to an opening within the company.

Thomas Moore

190 Barrow Road
Rosedale, AR 72201
(501)555-1234
TommyMoore@careercrib.com

May 21, 20XX

Dr. Joan Hartway
Customized Medical Training, Inc.
566 Stevens Street
Little Rock, AR 72212

Dear Dr. Joan Hartway:

Dave Gilbert recommended I send you my resume in reference to the Medical Illustrator position available in your multimedia department. It is my understanding that Mr. Gilbert spoke to you about my potential employment last week. I would like to highlight my qualifications for this position:

- Ability to illustrate in both traditional and computer-based mediums.
- Extensive training in illustrating human forms with advanced knowledge of the skeletal system.
- Advanced knowledge of the Adobe Creative Suite and Macromedia Flash.
- Great sense of design with a focus on usability and functionality.

While in school, I worked as a freelance portrait artist for three years. I am also the recipient of the "Portrait Scholarship for Illustrators," sponsored by the Illustrator's Society of America. The scholarship is only awarded to five recipients a year among over 1,000 applicants.

Since Dave Gilbert is already familiar with my work he can vouch for my work ethic and level of skill. I will call you next Friday to answer any questions you may have and set up a possible appointment to review my portfolio. Thank you for your time and consideration.

Sincerely,

Thomas Moore

Thomas Moore

FIGURE 5-7 Sample referral cover letter

Referral Letter

This referral letter directly relates a positive educational experience with a new potential job. The referrer had a positive experience with the author of the letter and suggested contacting a particular company. The letter then goes on to highlight the author's experience that will benefit the company.

1010 Highland Court
Memphis, TN 38101
(423)555-1234
GPenn@Careercrib.com

George Penn

December 18, 20XX

The Sound Lab
56 Dobler Road
Memphis, TN 38124
Attention: Michael Burnes

Dear Mr. Burnes:

I was referred to you by Anne Christopher who said you are in search of a highly proficient Assistant Audio Engineer. Anne Christopher was a guest lecturer in my Advanced Mixing class and she was very impressed with my level of Pro Tools knowledge. I am enclosing my resume and demo CD which highlights my experience and training.

As my resume demonstrates, I am well trained in Pro Tools, Logic, and several other cross-platform audio programs. I am also well trained in large format recording consoles including Neve, SSL, and Trident. My recording experience includes various styles of music including Rock, Hip Hop, Jazz, and live concerts. Additionally, my background includes ten years of musical training in piano and drums. I am very proficient in tuning drums and have advanced knowledge of music theory.

While in school, I have been employed as a work study and am in charge of running the recording studios during my assigned work hours. My duties included assisting students with class projects, scheduling lab time, and signing out microphones for recording sessions. Additionally, I volunteered to run live sound for various school theater productions that include musicals, dramas, and variety shows.

I will be graduating this spring, but I would like to start working as soon as a position is available. I am willing to perform any related duties assigned to get an opportunity to work in your recording studio. Please contact me at (423) 555-1234 or via e-mail at GPenn@careercrib.com to schedule an interview. If I have not heard from you by January 5th, I will call your office to answer any questions you may have.

Sincerely,

George Penn

George Penn

FIGURE 5-8 Sample referral cover letter

5.4.3 Cold Letter

The cold letter is probably the most difficult type of letter to get a positive response from. Considering the company might not have a job opening available, do not expect to get many responses. However, if there is a company you have always wanted to work for, you should still give it a try. You may also want to try to get a meeting with the company to network. If a job is not available, you can request a few minutes of their time to explore the industry. The key is to try and land face to face time with the company. Hopefully this will lead to a job in the future. Use the Worksheet in Figure 5–9 to help you draft a cold cover letter.

COLD LETTER WORKSHEET

Company Name: _____

Company Address: _____

_____

Contact Name or Addressee to Send Resume to: _____

Contact E-mail Address: _____

Contact Phone Number: _____

Department You Want to Wok for:_____

Position(s) Seeking: _____

Number of Years of Related Experience Required: _____

Why Do You Want to Work for the Company? _____

_____

_____

_____

_____

List of Computer Skills Required: _____

_____

List of Related Skills Required: _____

_____

List All of Your Software Skills That Apply to This Job: _____

_____

_____

_____

Summarize Your Related Skills and Other Personal Traits That Are Applicable to This Position: _____

_____

_____

_____

_____

FIGURE 5-9   Cold letter worksheet

Sample cold cover letters (Figures 5.10, 5.11, and 5.12)

Cold Letter

This is an introductory letter focusing on the author's passion for a specific industry. If a position is not available, it requests a meeting to explore possible industry options. The goal is to get a meeting with the recipient.

Kara Marie Pierce

19 Main Street
Kissimmee, FL 34755
(407)555-1234
KMP2366@Careercrib.com

April 19, 20XX

Mr. James Smith
ESPN
1 Media Way
Bristol CT, 06010

Dear Mr. Smith:

I will be graduating NYU this May with a Bachelor of Arts in Cinema Studies and would like to explore employment opportunities in Sports Broadcasting. As a student I produced a documentary entitled, "Basketball, The Street League," which focuses on inner-city basketball and its players.

I am inquiring about any entry-level positions that may be available at ESPN or its affiliates. I am willing to relocate and work any shift that is available. My passion for sports and broadcasting makes me an ideal candidate for ESPN. I am experienced in both ENG and Studio style production and am familiar with both video and film production techniques. Additionally, I have a great eye for editing and composition.

If a position is not currently available, I would like to request a few minutes of your time to seek your advice on entering the industry. I realize your time is limited and would keep the meeting brief. I would also like to send you a copy of my basketball documentary. It will be entered in several film festivals over the next year.

Enclosed is my resume. Please contact me at (407)555-1234. I am available for a meeting at your convenience.

Sincerely,

Kara Marie Pierce

Kara Marie Pierce

FIGURE 5-10   Sample cold cover letters

Cold Letter

This is an introductory letter focusing on the author's passion for a specific industry. If a position is not available, it requests a meeting to explore possible industry options. The goal is to get a meeting with the recipient.

Kristen Johnson

22 17th Avenue ~ Los Angeles, CA 90013 ~ (310)555-1234 ~
KJ19@Yahoo.com

July 29, 20XX

Ms. Gertrude Spelling
Art Department
Hallmark
P.O. Box 419034
Kansas City, MO 64141

Dear Ms. Spelling:

I am sending this letter and enclosed resume as an inquiry into possible openings in your Creative Department. I am seeking an Assistant Art Director Position and would like to request an interview to share my portfolio and ideas with your company. Your company's reputation for delivering the finest greeting cards and e-cards is unsurpassed in the industry. I feel I can contribute greatly to your Team.

While at Parsons, I was the Art Director for the school's art magazine and have also functioned as the webmaster and designer for several websites, which are listed on my enclosed resume. I am well skilled in Photoshop, Quark, InDesign, Illustrator, Dreamweaver, Flash, and Director. Additionally, my Art Directing experience and additional training at my internship at a large printing press company have given me advanced knowledge of preflighting artwork for print.

I will be in Kansas City from August 17th–August 28th and would like to meet with you. If those dates do not work, I can make other arrangements that are more convenient. I can be contacted at (310) 555-1234. I will contact you late next week to discuss possible vacancies and to set up a possible interview. If a position is not available at this time, I would still be interested in meeting with you to discuss any possible future openings.

Thank you for your time and consideration.

Sincerely,

Kristen Johnson

Kristen Johnson

FIGURE 5-11   Sample cold cover letters

Cold Letter

Although this letter is not in response to a job advertisement, the author is familiar with the company. He brings up his positive experience with the company as a reason for wanting to be employed there.

Jim Delphi

200 Carol Street ~ Plainview, NY 11803 ~ (516) 555-5555 ~ Jim@careercrib.com

June 16, 20XX

Dr. Hilton
Provost
Long Island Design School
1234 South Service Road
Melville, NY 11747

Dear Dr. Hilton:

As a former graduate of the Long Island Design School, it would be an honor to be employed as an instructor at your school. I have just completed my Master of Arts in Illustration and would be interested in becoming an adjunct or full-time instructor. I am available for the upcoming semester to teach classes in the following subjects:

- Studio classes in Illustration, 2D design, 3D design, and Typography.
- Computer classes in Photoshop, Illustrator, InDesign, Illustrator, Quark, Flash, and Fireworks.
- Art History and Modern Art.
- Web Design and Multimedia development.

I have extensive design and freelance experience in both traditional and digital mediums. My portfolio is available at: www.JimDelphi.com. Additionally, my recent pen and ink illustrations are on display at the Long Island Art leagues gallery in Huntington, New York. It will be available for viewing until July 15th.

I would greatly appreciate an opportunity to interview with you. Please contact me at (516) 555-5555. If I have not heard from you by June 30th, I will call your office to confirm you received this letter and enclosed resume.

Thank you for your time and consideration.

Sincerely,

Jim Delphi

Jim Delphi

FIGURE 5-12   Sample cold cover letter

Additional cover letter samples can be viewed at www.careercrib.com

REVIEW QUESTIONS/ACTIVITIES

1. Why is it important to research a company before drafting your cover letter?

2. List seven guidelines to effective cover letter writing.

3. Describe how your cover letter will vary depending on whether you are drafting a letter in response to a job advertisement, referral from an employee, or a cold letter.

The Job Interview

OUTLINE

OBJECTIVES

- Learn how to prepare for a job interview
- Research the company
- Learn how to dress for an interview
- Know what to bring to the interview
- Prepare for questions
- Prepare questions to ask
- Prepare proper methods to follow up a job interview

INTRODUCTION

Interviewing is a skill that all people can master with a little practice and preparation. There is no magic trick to acing an interview. It involves having confidence, being prepared, and displaying honesty. This chapter will focus on preparing for the interview, knowing what to do and not do in an interview, and determining how to follow-up.

6.1 PREPARING FOR A JOB INTERVIEW

Congratulations! You have been called for a job interview. Now what? The potential employer already has reviewed your resume and cover letter and thinks you may be a match for the company's vacancy. Now you need to secure the job through an interview. The best way to land the job is to research the company and figure out how your background fits the company's needs. Understanding their products, clients, corporate environment, and nature of their business is very important. With the proper research you will impress the employer and possibly secure a job offer.

Some information you should know about the company includes:

- What is the company's specialty?
- Who are their clients (past and present)?
- What is their target market?
- What should be known about the department you will be working in?
- Who are the company's competitors? What are their strengths and weaknesses?

6.1.1 Your Appearance

Unfortunately, we are often judged by our appearance, and we do not get a second chance to make a first impression. It is important to dress appropriately for a job interview. Knowing how to dress in a creative field can be tricky. As creative people, many employers do expect us to be a little more eccentric; however, you should still try to fit in to the corporate culture of the business.

When in doubt, it is better to overdress than underdress. You will never lose a prospective job by overdressing. For example, if the company's dress code is business casual and you show up in a suit and tie (men) or pant

> Nothing will impress the company more than demonstrating an extensive understanding of their business and client's needs.

suit with a nice button-down blouse (women), it will demonstrate to the employer that you are serious about the job. However, if you show up underdressed, it will appear as a lack of respect for the company or that you just do not care about the job.

Dressing Guidelines

Men	Women
Suit with a tie and matching shoes. Make sure you wear colored socks that match your suit.	Pant suit or a skirt that covers your knees. Wear a matching blouse. A jacket is always a nice touch.
Keep facial hair neat and trimmed.	Make sure your navel is covered.
Cover up tattoos and remove piercings. No tongue rings!	Cover up tattoos and remove excessive piercings. No tongue rings!

6.1.2 Things to Bring with You to the Job Interview

1. **Resume.** Bring additional copies of your resume printed on high quality paper. You should have at least three or four copies, as you may be interviewed by several people at once.

2. **Job application information.** You might be asked to fill out a job application. The application will probably request information such as the college's location and your graduation date from college, start and end dates of former jobs, and contact information and reference contact information. Make sure you have a list of all this information available.

3. **List of references.** Have a list of at least three references. Make sure the people listed know you will be listing them as a reference. You can also bring letters of recommendation and client testimonials including thank-you letters. Make sure your references are professional, not friends or family. Former and current employers, freelance clients, and teachers are strong professional references.

4. **Pen and paper.** You may need to take notes and (or) write down the names and contact information of the people you meet with. Also write down any questions that arise during the interview for you to ask when it is your turn for questions.

5. **Portfolio/demo reel.** Bring a print version of your portfolio. Make sure your prints are mounted properly and presented cleanly. Pay extra attention to detail. The employer will notice if your presentation is sloppy. You may also want to have additional

high quality copies to leave with the company. You can also bring a copy of your digital portfolio. If you are a digital artist, Web designer, film, video, audio, or any other designer that requires a digital portfolio, your presentation is equally important.

6. **List of questions and points to cover.** There is nothing wrong with bringing notes into the interview with you. Prepare a list of questions and points to cover. During the interview, you may refer to your sheet to make sure you cover all important points that you want to make as well as ask any questions that you may have. It is a good idea to have this list typed. It will demonstrate to the hiring manager the effort you put into your interview preparation.

6.2 BEING A PROFESSIONAL AND ACING THE INTERVIEW

Your first impression will set the tone for your interview. Therefore, you must present yourself as a professional from the moment you walk into the office. You already know what to bring and the type of preparation needed before arriving for the interview. Now you need to impress the interviewer with your professionalism and ability.

1. **Arrive ten to fifteen minutes early for the interview.** Do not arrive sooner than fifteen minutes early. Never arrive late! If something happens and you are going to arrive late, make sure you call and let the interviewer know why. Arriving late is probably the worst first impression you can make. Nobody wants to hire a person who cannot meet deadlines or who will not be punctual.

2. **Be courteous.** Every employee at that company from the secretary and janitor to the CEO should be treated with respect and politeness. In fact, the receptionist or secretary probably has more influence than most people at a company. The receptionist is the gatekeeper and can get you on the phone or your mail read by the hiring manager better than anybody else. Additionally, it is not uncommon for the hiring manager to ask the receptionist about your demeanor while waiting. The hiring manager knows you will try to be on your best behavior while in the interview. You are more likely to be yourself in the waiting area. If you were rude or spent your waiting time on your cell phone, the receptionist will share this information with the hiring manager.

3. **Patience.** It can be nerve racking waiting for the interviewer to call you in, but you must be patient. Do not spend your time playing video games on your Palm Pilot, talking on your cell phone, or doing anything else electronic. In fact, *MAKE SURE*

YOUR CELL PHONE IS OFF!!! Whatever else is going on in your life can wait until you leave the office. The best thing you can do while waiting for the interview is to sit up straight, be comfortable, and sit quietly. You can review your resume or company literature in the waiting room. Also take this time to rehearse your responses to common questions in your head (do not talk to yourself).

4. **Presentation.** Do not walk into the interview holding loose pieces of paper and looking disorganized. Your papers should be in a neat portfolio-type organizer. You do not need to have a briefcase, just a portfolio for your artwork (if applicable) and a portfolio-type organizer for your resume, list of references, notes, notebook, and pens.

5. **Etiquette.** There is conflicting arguments about offering to shake hands at an interview. The best way to approach the hand-shake is to make yourself available for a handshake but let the interviewer extend his or her hand first. When shaking hands, make sure your handshake is firm and your hand is not sweaty or dirty. Having a clammy, limp handshake will not make a good impression.

6. **Respect.** Demonstrate respect by addressing the interviewer by her last name. If she tells you to call her by her first name, then it is okay to do so. Also, wait until you are asked to sit. If the interviewer motions you to a chair, then of course you should sit.

7. **During the interview.**
   ✓ Let the interviewer set the tone of the interview. She will often start with a question such as, "Tell me about yourself?" or "Why do you want to work for this company?" (See section 6.3 to review typical interview questions and ways to approach the question.) When answering the question, be honest and confident in your answer.

   ✓ If you do not know the answer to a question, it is okay to ask for a little time to think about a question or let the interviewer know you will get back to her with an answer shortly. When you send a thank-you letter, you can elaborate on any questions that need clarification.

   ✓ Keep your answers direct and to the point. Do not go off on tangents. Once you have fully answered the question, stop talking. Let the interviewer give you the next question or a follow-up question to your answer.

   ✓ Give examples from your experience. For example, if the interviewer asks you, "How would you handle a client who is not sure what type of design they want?" you can respond by giving an actual scenario from a professional experience such as, *"When I was hired to design the website, www.albumgraphics.com, the client was not sure what links they were going to need or what type of design they wanted. The first thing I did was to sit down with the client and get a strong understanding of both their current business and where they were looking to grow. In addition to covering their current services, I wanted to ensure that the website was adaptable for their future use. Next I created a flowchart to demonstrate the navigation and reviewed it with the client. We also reviewed other websites that the client liked. After understanding the type of designs the client was favorable to, I created three different front pages for the client to choose from. We ended up combining a few ideas from each and came up with what you see now. This site is in my digital portfolio contained on this CD-ROM. (Hand them your CD-ROM.)"* Your example could also be a classroom situation with a teacher or another student.

✓ Ask questions when given the opportunity. (See section 6.4 to see a list of suggested questions.) Make sure to show an interest in the company and the potential job.

8. **The end of the interview.** Follow the same etiquette as stated in point 5 for shaking hands on the way out. Make sure to thank the interviewer for the opportunity of interviewing and for her time. Also, ask the interviewer for a business card. Make sure you get her mailing address, e-mail address, and telephone number for following up.

9. **Thank-you letter.** Within Twenty-four hours of the interview, send a thank-you letter reiterating your interest in the position and thanking the interviewer for her time. The thank-you letter is extremely important and has become standard practice. It demonstrates a sincere interest in the position and courteousness on your part. It is also a great opportunity to remind the interviewer of whom you are and why the company should hire you. (See section 6.7 for a complete overview of the thank-you letter and samples.)

10. **Following up.** After about ten business days, if you have not heard from the company you can follow up with a telephone call. This call should be courteous and brief. Let the interviewer know you are still interested in the position and that you wanted to check the status of the search. If you are not able to reach her on the phone or have already been corresponding with her through e-mail, you can send a brief e-mail of inquiry about the search status.

6.3 TYPICAL INTERVIEW QUESTIONS

There is no preset list of questions that you will be asked in an interview. The interviewer will ask you many questions that will vary in topic. Questions will usually fall into the following categories:

6.3.1 Direct Questions Related to Your Skills and Work Experience

These questions are designed to assess your skills and qualifications for the position. Questions of this nature include:

Tell me about yourself?

This may be the first question you are asked. The first word out of your mouth should not be *Uh or Um*. Be prepared to discuss your professional skills and experience. Do not talk about your first babysitting job or your personal life. The employer wants you to tell him why he should hire you. Focus your answer on your professionalism and abilities. You can discuss your most recent job and your positive experience. You can also discuss your education and other experiences that lend to the job. Try to address the needs of the company and the position with your answers. Demonstrate how your qualities will fill the company's needs and help the business grow.

Why do you want to work for this company?

This question gives you the perfect opportunity to discuss all of the great research you have completed in preparation for your interview. Companies want employees who believe in their business and who will become an asset. They do not want employees who are only there for a paycheck. Knowing a little history about the company and its clients will go a long way in impressing them.

If you were referred by a current employee, a client, or another associate, say something like, "I am looking for a position in which my input and hard work will be valued. Mr. Jones in your advertising department told me what a great place this is to work at and that this company values input from all employees regardless of their title. Additionally, this company's track record for delivering cutting edge designs and innovative marketing campaigns is something I could contribute to with much success."

Tell me about your current position. What is your title and your responsibilities?

Discuss your current job in a positive manner. Even if your current job is a part-time position that is not in the field you are interviewing for, go into detail about your responsibilities and try to relate them to the new position. For example, if you work in customer service, discuss how you are a strong problem solver and work well in satisfying customer needs.

Why are you leaving your current job? (Why did you leave your last job?)

Be cautious with this question. It is not a good idea to bash your current employer. If you do not get along with your current boss or co-workers, keep that information to yourself. The interviewer may think you are difficult to get along with. Discussing limited growth potential in your current position is acceptable. If you are a recent graduate and your current position is not in your field of study, then emphasize your desire to enter your field of study. Other possible answers include:

- I am in search of a more challenging position with growth potential.
- I was laid off when my department was eliminated (or outsourced).—*Make sure this is true before stating this fact.*
- Company cutbacks caused my position to be eliminated.
- I wanted to take my career in a different direction.
- I am looking for a position that is closer to my home.
- I was not looking for a new job, but your available position is an exact match to my skill set and career goals.
- I have just graduated college and am looking for a position that fits my educational background.

Whatever your answer, try to put a positive spin that is proactive in your job search. Remember, the industry is small and a lot of information is made public. Do not lie about your company eliminating a department if it is not true. The new company may have a relationship with your former employer and may be able to verify whether your department is still in existence.

Why were you fired?

This is a tough question to answer. If you were fired from your previous job, be prepared to answer this question. Try to emphasize how you have grown from this experience. Keep your answer brief and

---

PRACTICAL INTERVIEW TIP

Be honest. You should never lie or bad mouth your relationship with another industry professional. There is a good possibility the person conducting the interview knows the person you are speaking of. The industry is small. Do not burn bridges!

---

concise. Do not ramble on about a bad boss or nasty co-workers. Possible answers can include:

- I did not research the job well enough when I accepted the position and it was not a great match for my skills. This position is a much better match for the following reasons. . . .

- I had personal issues that interfered with my ability to perform my job adequately. Those issues have since been resolved and will not prevent me from performing my duties in the future.

- A new manager took over my department and brought in his (her) own team. This has given me a chance to re-evaluate my career goals and focus them on pursuing opportunities that better fit my background.

What was the biggest challenge of your position and how did you overcome the challenge?

This question is designed to measure your adaptability and problem-solving skills. Try to think of a challenge that you encountered in which you had a positive outcome. Be specific in your details. For example, "My company was having difficulty staying current on technology. Some of our clients were requesting that we accept files from InDesign and we only accepted Quark Xpress files. I took it upon myself to buy a book on InDesign and trained my co-workers."

Describe your current relationship with your boss and your co-workers.

Keep this answer positive. If your boss is difficult, you can state that your boss is challenging, but describe how you effectively work with him or her. Speak of your ability to work as a team or individually. You may mention how you mentored another employee or worked together with a co-worker to conquer a problem.

How do your skills and training fit this position?

This is an open-ended question that gives you a lot of flexibility to answer. Use this chance to highlight your technical and design skills.

PRACTICAL INTERVIEW TIP

Do not be afraid to ask for a moment to consider your answer. Take your time to answer questions with thought. Do not just blurt out answers without thinking. Employers would rather see you take your time and evaluate your response. This might impress the interviewer more than your answer.

Directly relate your skills to the company's needs based upon your research and the job posting.

What unique experience can you bring to this position?

Use this question to discuss a unique ability that might help the company increase their productivity. Keep your answer professional, constructive, and job focused.

What is your biggest weakness?

This classic question is also one of the most difficult to answer. Do not say, "I am a workaholic." This is the most cliché answer you can give. Everybody likes to say this.

One technique is to mention a weakness that is not related to your duties for the job you are interviewing for. Another suggestion is to mention a weakness that you have developed a strong work around for. For example, "My handwriting is not that good, but I have developed very strong typing skills."

6.3.2 Questions About Your Career Goals and Future

Where do you see yourself in five years (ten years, etc.)?

Whatever you say, do not state that you want the interviewer's job. Maybe your goal is to be an Art Director or Supervisor; however, you do not want to come off as a threat to the person who is interviewing you. Be realistic in your goals. An answer that explains duties that you want to perform versus the title you want is a better way to approach answering the question. You may also give examples of things you would like to accomplish. Make sure that your answer is focused and direct. Do not say, "I don't know."

Have you applied for any other jobs?

Obviously, if you are serious about looking for a job, you have applied to other companies. Do not lie. State that you are actively searching for a job that fits your talents. However, be enthusiastic about the job that you are interviewing for. Be confident with the job at hand and let the employer know you are serious about working for the company. Employers

---

PRACTICAL INTERVIEW TIP

Bring a bottle of water with you. When you need an extra moment to think of an appropriate answer to a question, take a sip of water. This will give you a few extra seconds to evaluate your answer.

---

want to hire people who want to work for their company. They do not want to hire somebody who is just biding time until a better offer comes along.

What salary are you looking for? (See Chapter 7 if the employer is making you an offer.)

Before going on the interview, make sure you have completed some market research and know what the typical salary is for a similar position. Additionally, be familiar with what type of benefits package is usually offered with such a position and its value. If this question is asked early on in the interview and the company is not officially making an offer, there are a few ways to respond to this question (remember, you haven't been offered the position yet):

- Ask the interviewer, "What is the salary range for the position?"
- You can also emphasize, "Although money is important, the position and working for this company is my primary goal and I am sure you will treat me fair."
- "My salary requirements are in line with similar positions in the field. However, before I can give you a specific figure, I would need to know what type of benefits you are offering, a list of responsibilities for the job, and what type of schedule I will have." *Jobs that require a night shift or weekend hours usually pay more than a standard nine–five shift.*
- In the case of an employer wanting you to state a number after giving one of the previous responses, use your market research to give a wage that is competitive for the position. You may also state that you need health insurance coverage in addition to your wage.

The bottom line is you cannot give an exact figure without knowing the full compensation package. Benefits such as health insurance, dental insurance, vision plans, retirement plans (yes, you need to start thinking about retirement plans as a new graduate entering the workforce), bonuses, life insurance, vacation days, sick days, personal days, stock options (if they are a publicly traded company), profit sharing, long-term disability, and short-term disability are many of the benefits that companies offer and are part of your compensation. If these benefits are not covered by your employer, you must provide them for yourself. This must be factored into your decision to accept an offer for employment. (*For more information on benefits, see negotiating your salary in Chapter 7.*)

6.3.3 Questions to Evaluate Your Thought Process, Problem-Solving Skills, and Questions that Explore Your Personality

What was the last book you read for pleasure?

You might wonder why the interviewer is asking you this. He is trying to explore your personality. Employers want to make sure you have other interests outside of your work. Additionally, they do not want to hire a couch potato. Employers want literate employees who can spend time reading a book and exploring new ideas.

What accomplishments are you most proud of?

Try to keep this answer career focused. Maybe you are most proud of your ability to skateboard or surf, but that probably will not help get you the job unless the company you are interviewing with works in that industry. Try to focus on an accomplishment that may lend to the job requirements. If you are new to the industry and a recent graduate, speak of an academic accomplishment. Maybe you graduated with a high GPA or won a creative award for your designing skills. These are things you should focus on.

How would your co-workers describe you?

Discuss your ability to work in a team, meet deadlines, and be dependable. Employers are looking for candidates that will fit well into their company's environment. Use this question as an opportunity to discuss your ability to be part of a bigger team.

They may ask you situational problem-solving questions such as, "What would you do if a client calls and complains about . . .?"

This question gives you a great opportunity to demonstrate your customer service skills. Depending on the problem, use your reasoning skills to come up with an appropriate answer. The employer wants to see that you can handle a client and defuse a touchy situation. Emphasize your listening skills and demonstrate a methodical way of working with the client. The bottom line is the new employer wants to keep its customers happy. For example, if the client complained about their website not working properly in a specific browser, you may want to explore the issue while on the phone with the client. If the client has a legitimate issue, let the client know you understand their issue

---

PRACTICAL INTERVIEW TIP

If asked a question that you do not know the answer to, do not lie or make-up an answer. Tell the interviewer that you would need to do a little research or think about that question. Then, address the question in your thank-you letter or with a follow-up phone call within twenty-four hours of the interview.

---

and will bring it to the development team's attention. Take down the client's contact information and give them a time table of when you will contact them.

6.4 ASKING QUESTIONS IN THE INTERVIEW

It is very important that you prepare a few questions to ask during the interview. This demonstrates a genuine interest in the company and also demonstrates your thought process. It is not uncommon for the questions you are asking to make a greater impression than the answers you gave during their series of questions. This is another area where your research about the company will be very useful. Obviously, the more you know about the company and its clients, the better prepared you will be to ask questions.

Choose your questions wisely. Do not ask questions that have already been answered during the interview unless you want to explore that area more. You do not want to look like you were not listening earlier in the interview. Make sure the questions you are asking are not frivolous; they should have a relevant point. Questions can be focused on the job and its responsibilities, the company's culture, and the next steps in the interviewing process.

6.4.1 Sample Questions to Ask in the Interview

- What would be my day-to-day responsibilities?
- What goals would I be expected to accomplish in the first six months and year on the job?
- What are some of the department's ongoing and anticipated special projects?
- What software and current technologies are you currently using?
- If I am successful in this position, is there opportunity to grow?
- How will my performance be evaluated?
- What direction is the company going in?

- When do you expect to make a decision about this position?
- What is the next step in the interview process?
- What is your most pressing need to be filled by this position?
- What are some of the challenges I will face in this position?
- Does management have an open door policy for sharing new ideas?

6.5 QUESTIONS NOT TO ASK IN THE INTERVIEW

There are several things you should never ask during the initial interview. Many questions are better suited for asking when a job offer is being made. Here is a list of questions that should not be asked during the interview or should be held off until a job offer is being made:

What is the salary of the position?

Obviously you want to know how much a job pays. However, you should not ask this during the first interview unless they are offering you the job. Asking about salary this early in the interview process puts you at a disadvantage. The employer has not picked a final candidate and by asking salary at this point, you will not get their best offer. If you seem okay with the range that they may share with you, there is little room to bargain when they offer you the position. An exception to this rule is when the employer asks you, "What salary are you looking for?" *(See section 6.3.2)*

What business is this company in?

You should know what the company does before going into the interview.

The following questions should be saved for once the company has offered you the position. Asking them before a job offer is made makes you appear less interested in the company and self-centered. The company wants to hire somebody who is not just looking for a paycheck, but a person who wants to be part of their company. Do not ask these questions until a job offer has been made:

- How many sick, personal, and vacation days will I receive?
- When will I be eligible for a raise?
- Is my schedule flexible?
- What benefits am I entitled to?
- Am I eligible for overtime pay?

- How many hours a week do I need to work?
- How long is my lunch break?

All of these questions are legitimate and are important information when choosing to accept a job offer. However, wait for the appropriate time to address these issues. You will be in a much better position to negotiate when the company has chosen you over the other candidates they are interviewing.

6.6 ILLEGAL QUESTIONS — WHAT AN EMPLOYER CANNOT ASK

According to the **Equal Employment Opportunity Commission (EEOC)** (http://www.eeoc.gov), there are several laws that make it illegal to discriminate during the hiring process.

- **The Civil Rights Act of 1964** (Title VII) makes it illegal to discriminate in hiring practices based on race, color, religion, sex, and national origin.

- **The Age Discrimination in Employment Act of 1967** makes it illegal to discriminate in hiring practices based on age against persons who are forty years of age or older.

- Title I of the **Americans with Disabilities Act of 1990 (ADA)** makes it illegal to discriminate in hiring practices based on a disability.

The following have been deemed as illegal questions because asking these questions could potentially make the company vulnerable to a possible discrimination complaint and lawsuit:

1. What is your marital status? *A potential employer cannot ask any question pertaining to your marital status. This information can only be asked after a job has been offered and accepted for tax and benefit purposes only.*

2. Do you have children or people who are dependent on you for care? *After a job is accepted, an employer can ask you how many dependants you have for tax and insurance purposes.*

3. Are you pregnant or are you planning on starting a family soon? *An employer may be hesitant to hire a woman who is pregnant or starting a family soon because they do not want them to leave after only a few months. High employment turnover or maternity leave can be very expensive for an employer; however, the employer cannot discriminate against you based upon your family plans.*

4. How old are you? *An employer can only ask if your age meets the requirements for employment.*

5. Have you ever been arrested? *An employer can only ask, "Have you ever been convicted of a crime?" The only exceptions are jobs in law enforcement and jobs that require government security clearance.*

6. What is your ethnic background or country of origin? *An employer can ask if you are a legal U.S. resident or if you have a legal work visa.*

7. What is your religion or your religious practices? *Any question that inquires about your religious practices including holidays celebrated is illegal.*

8. Are you disabled and what is your medical history? *An employer can ask if you can perform certain work-related duties such as, "Can you lift at least fifty pounds?" They may also ask you, "Based upon the job as described, are there any job functions that you cannot perform"?*

6.6.1 Responding to an Illegal Question

Handling an illegal question can be a very tricky situation. In most cases, the question was probably asked out of ignorance and is not malice. Your response should be appropriate to the intentions of the interviewer. Your best response is to rephrase your answer into one of the legal versions of the illegal question. For example, if you are asked, "Do you have any children or people who depend on you for day-to-day care?" your response could be something like, "If you are asking me if I have any issues that would prevent me from performing my job duties, I do not."

Another option is to point out to the interviewer that the question is not appropriate for a job interview. However, this method may not benefit you in the end. You certainly do not want to turn the interview into an adversarial situation. Your best bet may be to just answer the question, especially if you think your answer will not hurt you. Nevertheless, be cautious in your approach.

Just because you are asked an illegal question does not mean that you didn't get the job because of your answer. Likewise, being asked an illegal question does not mean you were discriminated against. You would have to be able to prove discrimination if you want to take legal action against a company.

"WHAT DO I DO IF I HAVE BEEN DISCRIMINATED AGANIST DURING AN INTERVIEW?"

If you suspect that you have been the victim of discrimination or sexual harassment in the workplace, you should consult an attorney and (or) file a complaint with the U.S. Equal Employment Opportunity Commission (EEOC). To contact the EEOC, visit the website at: http://www.eeoc.gov, or call them at: 1-800-669-4000.

6.7 THANK YOU LETTERS

THANK-YOU LETTER ETIQUETTE

Make sure to send a thank-you letter to all of the people you interviewed with. Additionally, send your letters out within twenty-four hours of your interview.

After completing an interview, make sure to follow up with a thank-you letter. The thank-you letter is not optional. It has become expected and is a major part of the interviewing process. If the job selection comes down to two candidates, the person who follows up with a letter will get the job over the person who did not every time.

In addition to making a great impression, the thank-you letter can serve many purposes:

- It reminds the employer that you are a great candidate and reiterates your strong capabilities.
- It demonstrates your strong communication skills and writing ability.
- It provides follow up with any information you told the interviewer that you would get back to her on.
- It readdresses any questions that you did not answer fully and clearly or would like to elaborate on.

The format of your letter should follow a standard business letter style and include the following information:

1. **Top of the letter:**
   a. Your address, telephone number, and e-mail address
   b. Date
   c. Company's address
   d. Greeting (e.g., Dear Mrs. Smith:)

2. **Opening paragraph:**
   a. Thank the interviewer for his time.
   b. Remind the interviewer of the date and the position you interviewed for.
   c. Reiterate your interest in the position.

3. **Second paragraph** (and if necessary the third paragraph). The second paragraph should contain information that is specific to

your interview and how you fit the job. Consider one of the following themes for the paragraph:

a. Discuss a point that you forgot to mention or did not cover well in the interview and relate it to the job requirements. For example, *"After reviewing my notes from the job interview I have a much better understanding of your needs and would like to point out my strong project management skills. In addition to working as a design team member, I have worked directly with clients and have the ability to oversee projects. Furthermore, I have the ability to complete a project within a given budget and timeframe."*

b. Bring up something discussed during the interview and share your enthusiasm for the topic. For example, *"I am particularly impressed with your new Web-based streaming video initiative for your publishing library. This is the exact type of project I have been looking to get involved in. My advanced Web design skills and three years experience in preparing streaming media could be an asset for your company. I have extensive knowledge in streaming media formats and keep current on new trends in delivering content over the Web."*

c. Discuss the strong rapport you felt with the interviewer or team of interviewers (before discussing this, be confident that the feeling was mutual). For example, *"I truly enjoyed our time together and felt a great rapport with your entire team during the interview. Although our interview was short, I can already tell that I am an ideal candidate to join your team and would enjoy working with your staff. Your new team's desire to reinvent the company's brand and industry perception is a project I can contribute greatly to. As we discussed, my minor in marketing and recent internship at an advertising agency gives me additional knowledge that can benefit your long-term goals for this project."*

d. Discuss your ability to fill the company's immediate needs. For example, *"During our interview we discussed how the video editing department will be switching over to the latest versions of Final Cut Pro. I would like to point out that in addition to my strong technical and creative background in video editing, I also have the ability to assist in the training of your current staff in Final Cut Pro. During my fours years of college, I worked as a peer tutor training other students in the advanced features of Final Cut Pro. Additionally, I have extensive experience in using Garage Band and can assist in the production of musical scores for your productions."*

4. **Last paragraph.** Sum up your letter by showing appreciation for the employer's time, reiterating your interest in the position in the company, and that you look forward to hearing from them about the position.

SHOULD YOU E-MAIL OR MAIL YOUR THANK-YOU LETTER?

There are arguments both for and against using either traditional mail or e-mail to send your thank-you letter. Traditional mail is certainly more formal and allows you to add your signature. Additionally, it requires more effort to open the letter, which as a result may make your letter taken a little more seriously than an e-mail. However, the e-mail will arrive the same day as your interview and shows the most diligence.

You might want to base which format you choose by the type of correspondence and pre-interview atmosphere that surrounded the interview. If applications for the job and follow-up correspondence were communicated through e-mail, it is certainly acceptable to use e-mail to send your thank-you letter. Conversely, if you mailed or faxed your resume any did not have any e-mail correspondence with the employer, you are probably better off sending a traditional letter.

Another tactic is to cover both bases by e-mailing your thank-you letter and sending a copy via traditional mail. You can even make a note at the bottom of the e-mail that a hard copy of the letter has been sent by mail. Either way, make sure your thank-you letter follows the proper letter format and mailed copies are printed on a high quality paper with a matching envelope.

5. **Signature.** Make sure to sign your letter with either "Thank you" or "Sincerely." Next, sign your name and print it below your signature. If you are e-mailing your thank-you letter, obviously you will not be able to sign it, but you should still keep a professional business letter format.

Sample Thank You Letters (Figures 6–1 and 6–2)

Melissa Smith

211 5th Avenue · Boston, MA 02331 · (415) 555-5555 ·
e-mail: M_Smith@Pratt.edu

June 21, 20XX

James Washington
Website Innovators, INC.
1234 Brewster Street
Boston, MA 02335

To Mr. Washington:

I would like to thank you for taking the time to interview me today for the Web Designer position. I found the interview process to be a positive experience and I am very impressed with the company.

I am particularly impressed with your new Web-based streaming video initiative for your publishing library. This is the exact type of project I have been looking to get involved in. My advanced Web design skills and three years experience in preparing streaming media could be an asset for your company. I have extensive knowledge in streaming media formats and keep current on new trends in delivering content over the Web.

I would like to reiterate my interest in this position. I can assure you that I will put my best effort forward and live up to your high level of standards for this position. If I can provide you with any further information, please contact me at (415) 555-5555 or M_Smith@Pratt.edu. I look forward to hearing from you in the near future.

Thank you again for your time and consideration.

Sincerely,

Melissa Smith

Melissa Smith

FIGURE 6-1   Melissa Smith

Andrew Jones
37 West John Street · Chicago, IL 60605 · 708.555.5555 ·
e-mail: Andy_Jones@Careercrib.com

April 12, 20XX

Jocelyn Jennings
Retro Gaming Unlimited
1223 5th Avenue
New York, NY 10014

Dear Ms. Jocelyn Jennings:

I greatly enjoyed our meeting this past Wednesday about the editing position in your animation department. I was particularly impressed with the
tour of the facility you gave me and enjoyed meeting your design team.

During our interview we discussed how the department will be switching
over to the latest version of Final Cut Pro. I would like to point out that
in addition to my strong technical and creative background in video
editing, I also have the ability to assist in the training of your current
staff in Final Cut Pro. During my four years of college, I worked as a peer
tutor training other students in the advanced features of Final Cut Pro.
Additionally, I have extensive experience in using Garage Band and can
assist in the production of musical scores for your productions.

Your team is extraordinarily talented and demonstrated a great rapport.
I am sure if given this opportunity I will be able to work well with your
team and become a great addition that will help increase productivity.
I look forward to hearing from you soon.

Thank you for your time and consideration.

Sincerely,

Andrew Jones

Andrew Jones

FIGURE 6-2   Andrew Jones

FOLLOW-UP PHONE CALL

So you have sent a thank-you note and have not heard back from the company yet. This is not uncommon. After about two weeks, it is perfectly acceptable and recommended that you call the interviewer. When calling, be courteous and restate your interest in the position. Then ask, "What is the status of the search to fill the position?"

You may also ask when they except to make a decision. It is okay to let them know you are interested in working for the company, but do not come off as desperate. There is a fine line between being enthusiastic and coming off as desperate. If they state a decision will not be made for a given time period, ask what is the best way to follow up with them going forward.

6.8 HANDLING REJECTION

Getting rejected is never easy. Unfortunately, it is a part of the interviewing process. You want to use rejections as a learning and growth exercise. Try to get feedback from the company as to why you did not receive the position. Most companies won't give you feedback other than to say they had a stronger candidate, but you may get lucky. Ask the interviewer what areas you can improve on so you may be a better candidate next time. Do not argue with their response. Thank them for their candor and use this experience as a growth exercise for next time.

Do not take rejection personally. It is possible that you did nothing wrong, but that another person they interviewed was just a stronger candidate. Creative fields are highly competitive and you must be patient in your job search. The most important thing to remember is to believe in yourself and keep trying. Use each interview as a growth exercise and as practice for your next interview. If you stay consistent with your job search, you will land a job that fits you.

CAREER TIP

It is important to always continue developing your trade. While searching for a job and even after you land one, continue to practice your craft and keep current on industry trends. As you develop, your value will increase and you will become more valuable to an employer. Staying current on trends includes keeping current on both new software releases and creative trends in the industry. Your best source for this information is industry magazines.

PRACTICE INTERVIEW TIP

When performing a peer interview, try videotaping the interview. Observe your body language and your reaction to certain questions.

REVIEW QUESTIONS/ACTIVITIES

Peer Interview

- Break into groups of two and practice interviewing each other. Use sample questions from this chapter and keep track of each other's answers.
- Dress appropriately for the peer interview.
- Draft a thank-you letter thanking the interviewer for the interview.

1. What type of information should you know about a company before going on the interview?
2. List three questions you should not ask during an interview and describe why.
3. List the three laws that apply to discrimination during the hiring process.
4. Describe the proper attire for a job interview.

CHAPTER 7

Congratulations! You Have Been Offered a Job!

OUTLINE

OBJECTIVES

- Negotiate a salary
- Understand your benefits
- Write acceptance letters
- Reject a job offer
- Adapt to your new working environment
- Maintain a positive attitude

INTRODUCTION

Few things in your professional career are as exciting as receiving your first real job offer in your chosen field. It is difficult to get that first break in the field, but you are taking the first step now. However, before we jump at a job offer, we need to understand everything that is part of it. Is the position full-time or part-time? What hours are you expected to work? Does this position offer benefits? What do these benefits do for me? Who will be my supervisor? What type of environment will I be working in?

If the job is a standard full-time position, you will be working at that job forty hours a week. In creative fields, you may be working a longer week with strange hours. If you are working in film production, your shift might start at 4 a.m. and end at 11 p.m. If you are working at a magazine or newspaper publication, you may not be able to go home until the copy goes to print. Although you may have to sacrifice some of your personal life to succeed in this industry, few careers are as satisfying as being creative for a living.

7.1 THE JOB OFFER

As discussed in chapter 6, you do not want to discuss salary until the employer broaches the topic. During a second or third interview, the employer may discuss your salary requirements or make you an offer. It is best to try and get the employer to offer the first number. (See chapter 6, "What salary are you looking for?") There is a difference between being asked what type of salary you are looking for and getting a job offer.

Either during a follow-up interview or shortly after, the company will make you an offer if they want to hire you. Do not jump at the first offer. Any ethical company will give you time to consider the offer. If they require an answer on the spot, consider if this is the type of company you want to work for. Ask them, "When do you need an answer by?" or "Can I get back to you within forty-eight hours?" This decision is very important and you should take a day or two to consider the offer.

7.1.1 How Much Should You Get Paid?

How much money you should expect to get paid in an entry-level position is going to vary greatly based on the position, your skill set, and the geographical region. Before you go on an interview, you should do some research on salaries in your area. There are many sources you can use. One method is to search for similar jobs in the same region. Often the salary range will be listed in the job advertisements. Table 7.1 shows several websites that offer this information. Many of these websites will provide a free basic report and charge a fee for an advanced report. With a little research, you should be able to get this information for free.

TABLE 7–1 Salary Research Sources

Website	Description
www.bls.gov	**U.S. Department of Labor—Bureau of Labor Statistics**. This includes salary statistics, job descriptions, local and national labor statistics, salary calculators, and a wealth of other resources. This is the first place you should start your salary research. The information is free.
www.designersalaries.com	**AIGA (American Institute of Graphic Arts)/Aquent—Survey of Design Salaries**. This surveys jobs in the graphic design field and is conducted annually, broken down by job title and location. The information is free.
www.jobstar.org	**JobStar Central**. Free links to hundreds of salary surveys; also has many other career searching resources.
www.careerjournal.com	**Career Journal (The Wall Street Journal)**. This includes negotiation tips, salary research, articles, advice, and many other great resources.
www.salary.com	**Salary.com**. Free basic salary reports based upon the job title, experience, and geographical location. Premium report is available for a fee. Many other tools and articles are available.
www.payscale.com	**PayScale.com**. Free basic salary reports based upon the job title, experience, and geographical location. Premium report is available for a fee. Many other tools and articles are available.

7.1.2 Consider the Whole Package

When evaluating a job offer there are many things to consider. Obviously the first thing most people want to know is what salary the company is offering. However, you need to look at the whole package. Consider the following questions:

- What are the benefits?
- How much of a contribution will you have to make to your benefits (i.e. health insurance, long-term disability, etc.)?
- Who will be your supervisor?
- What will your work environment be?
- What will your schedule be (hours, days, etc.)?
- Is there room for growth?
- What type of projects will you be working on?
- How long is your commute?

- What will your traveling expenses cost you?
- How much vacation time will you be entitled to?

These factors should play an important role in your decision whether or not to accept a job. As a recent graduate, you may never have been concerned with benefits such as health insurance, retirement accounts, and disability insurance. It is time to start thinking of these things now. Your benefits package has a value and you need to factor this into your job offer's value. For example, health insurance is very expensive to get on your own. It can cost you anywhere from $200 to $600 per month to purchase on your own; perhaps even more if you have a family. If your job offers health insurance, then the compensation package is worth more than just the salary amount alone. Conversely, if the compensation package is strictly monetary and no benefits are included, that means you will have to obtain health insurance and other benefits on your own. Deduct this expense from your salary to estimate the true value of the job offer.

7.2 BENEFITS

Benefits and their value are a huge part of your compensation package. Not all of the benefits listed in this section will be offered by every employer. Review this list and figure out which benefits are necessities and which benefits are nice perks.

7.2.1 Health Insurance

The most important benefit you will need is health insurance. Potentially, the biggest financial mistake you can make is not having health insurance. The cost of not having health insurance can impact your financial health for the rest of your life. Hopefully you will never need your health insurance beyond an annual checkup. However, if you are ever ill, need to stay in a hospital, and have surgery, the bills can run into hundreds of thousands of dollars. Not having health insurance could leave you in debt for the rest of your life. You will be paying old hospital bills instead of making a mortgage payment. Additionally, this amount of debt can ruin your credit rating and possibly cause you to file for bankruptcy. Furthermore, not having health insurance limits your options for potential life-saving medical procedures and may prevent you from receiving the best medical care.

Often employees have to make a partial contribution to the cost of health insurance. Most employers will pay a large percentage such as Two-Thirds of the total cost of the insurance premium leaving the employee to pay the last One-Third. The employee's contribution to the health insurance premium is tax deductible and is automatically deducted from your paycheck from pre-tax dollars. Whether or not the employee has to make a contribution and how much it is will vary by the employer's company policy. This is certainly a factor when evaluating a compensation package.

In addition to considering your required contribution to a health plan, you must also consider the type of coverage and the insurance company. Types of plans and the insurance provider will vary in quality substantially and will have a different value to you. The number of doctors and whether your current doctor accepts the plan should also be considered when evaluating the health plan.

Understanding Insurance Terms

(Adapted from: *Checkup on Health Insurance Choices*. AHCPR Publication No. 93-0018, December 1992. Agency for Health Care Policy and Research, Rockville, MD. http://www.ahrq.gov/consumer/insuranc.htm. Used with permission.)

- **Coinsurance.** In certain medical plans such as fee-for-service, the patient is required to pay a certain amount of the medical bills. This is often a percentage such as 30 percent. In this case, the insurance company pays 70 percent and the patient will pay 30 percent of the medical expenses. Your coinsurance contributions are usually limited to a maximum out-of-pocket expense.

- **Coordination of benefits.** A system to eliminate duplication of benefits when you are covered under more than one group plan. Benefits under the two plans usually are limited to no more than 100 percent of the claim.

- **Copayment.** After you have paid your deductible, most insurance companies will require you to make a copayment toward each doctor's visit and prescription purchase. For example, when visiting the doctor you may have to pay $15 toward the visit. The health insurance company will pay the rest of the fee. If that doctor writes you a prescription, you may have to pay $20 toward that prescription and the health insurance company will pay the rest. The copayment amounts will vary depending on the health insurance coverage.

- **Covered expenses.** Most insurance plans, regardless of the type of plan, do not pay for all medical services. Some may not pay for prescription drugs. Others may not pay for mental health care. Covered services are those medical procedures the insurer agrees to pay for. They are listed in the policy. Make sure to review this information when evaluating a plan and its value.

- **Deductible.** This is the amount of money you must pay each year to cover your medical care expenses before your insurance policy starts paying. For example, the health insurance provider may require you to pay a $500 deductible per person and $1,000 deductible per family. This means patients must pay the first $500 of their health costs. After the patient pays the $500, the health insurance coverage will start paying toward the patient's health care based upon the terms of the plan. The $1,000 deductible per family means, if you have four people in your family, each person's deductible is $500 until the entire family has paid $1,000. Once the family has paid the family amount, the health insurance coverage will cover all family members regardless of whether or not that family member has paid the full $500 toward their health costs.

- **Exclusions.**   These are specific conditions or circumstances for which the policy will not provide benefits. Usually, non-essential, cosmetic surgery such as facelifts and liposuction would not be covered.

- **Managed care.**   This includes ways to manage costs, use, and quality of the healthcare system. All HMOs, PPOs and many fee-for-service plans have managed care.

- **Maximum out-of-pocket expense.**   This is the maximum amount of money you will be required to pay toward your medical expenses in a given year. After the maximum has been paid out, the insurance company will cover 100 percent of what they consider to be the reasonable and customary cost for the treatment. You are no longer responsible for the coinsurance and deductibles.

- **Noncancelable policy.**   This is a policy that guarantees you can receive insurance, as long as you pay the premium. It is also called a guaranteed renewable policy.

- **Preexisting condition.**   This is a health problem that existed before the date your insurance became effective. It is not uncommon for a health insurance company to exclude coverage for preexisting conditions for a waiting period up to twelve months when the patient has not had health insurance in the past twelve months. You need to get health insurance when you are healthy. If you have insurance and are switching companies or you are starting a new job, the "preexisting condition clause" is waived and you can enroll with full coverage.

- **Premium.**   This is a fee paid for insurance by you and (or) your employer, usually paid monthly for health insurance.

- **Primary care doctor.**   This is usually your first contact for health care. Although often a family physician or internist, some women use their gynecologist. A primary care doctor monitors your health, diagnoses and treats minor health problems, and refers you to specialists if another level of care is needed. This is often called a gatekeeper doctor. Certain plans such as HMOs require you to visit your primary care doctor before seeing a specialist in non-emergency situations.

- **Provider.**   A provider is any person (doctor, nurse, dentist) or institution (hospital or clinic) that provides medical care.

- **Third-party payer.** A Third-party payer is any payer for health-care services other than you. This can be an insurance company, an HMO, a PPO, or the federal government.

- **In-network coverage.** This is a preapproved list of doctors that are covered by the health insurance. Some plans limit patients to in-network doctors only. When visiting in-network doctors, patients are only required to pay the copay or predefined percentage of the contracted amount.

- **Out-of-network coverage.** Many health insurance plans allow patients to visit doctors that are not in-network, but will cover the costs at a lower rate. Additionally, fees charged by these doctors may exceed what the health insurance companies consider to be the customary and reasonable charge for the medical service. The insurance company will only pay based on this amount and your doctor will require the patient to pay the difference. Although out-of-network coverage is more expensive, it gives the patient the most flexibility when choosing doctors.

Different types of health insurance plans

- **Fee-for-service.** This type of plan has great flexibility, but will also cost you more money. It is often referred to as traditional health insurance. In this type of plan there is usually an annual deductible, and then the insurance company will pay a percentage of the covered medical expenses. For example, the patient would pay the first $500 of medical expenses and then 20 percent of future expenses. The insurance company pays 80 percent of the covered costs after the deductible has been met.[1]

- **Health Maintenance Organization (HMO).** A type of managed health care that costs the patient less money, but also has limitations on the coverage. HMOs require patients to use doctors in a preselected network of physicians and hospitals. Patients must choose a primary physician, often referred to as a gatekeeper doctor. All medical treatment is managed through the primary physician. If the patient needs to see a specialist, the patient needs to obtain a referral from this primary physician. Although the coverage is limited to the network and needs referrals, the costs associated are much less expensive. The patient is usually responsible for a small copayment ranging from $5 to $25 per doctor's visit regardless of the procedures performed. Prescription drugs are also covered with a similar copayment requirement. When given a choice of health plans, make sure you check the network to make sure your doctors and area hospitals are included in the network.

---

[1] Health insurance. (n.d.). *Gale Encyclopedia of Cancer.* Retrieved August 04, 2007, from Answers.com website: http://www.answers.com/topic/health-insurance

- **Preferred Provider Organization (PPO).** A PPO plan is a managed healthcare plan with more flexibility than a HMO. It still has a network of physicians and hospitals for the patient to choose from, but there is no need to pick a primary physician or get referrals. You may choose anybody in the network including a specialist and still pay only the deductible. You also have flexibility to go out of the network, but your out-of-network coverage will be covered similar to a fee-for-service plan. There is usually a deductible and then the insurance company will pay a percentage of your covered healthcare costs. Although this plan is usually more expensive than an HMO, it provides the insured with the most flexible coverage while still keeping costs manageable. When given a choice between an HMO and a PPO, the PPO will protect you better and give you the flexibility of seeing any doctor you want in case of a severe medical condition.

- **Point-of-service (POS).** POS plans are HMOs with additional out-of-network coverage. Patients are still required to choose a primary care physician and obtain referrals to see a specialist; however, they also have out-of-network coverage like the fee-for-service plan. When you visit your primary physician and obtain referrals, you are only responsible for the copayment. If you go out-of-network or see a doctor without a referral you are responsible for a deductible and a percentage of the medical costs.[2]

- **Health Reimbursement Account (HRA).** An HRA is a consumer-driven plan that has similar in-network and out-of-network coverage as a PPO plan. However, this plan differs from a PPO because of its large deductible and reimbursement account set up by your employer. The health insurance coverage is often 100 percent of covered medical costs after the insured pays the deductible. The deductible is large such as $1,500 per person for in-network and $3,000 per person out-of-network; however, your employer sets up a reimbursement account to cover a portion of the deductible. For example, your employer may cover the first $1,000 of medical expenses for the year, you are responsible for the next $500 and then the insurance company covers the rest of your covered medical expenses for the rest of the year. Many employers will allow unused money to rollover into future years.

  Because of the large deductible, the premium is significantly less than the other health plans. The difference is so significant that it is more cost effective for your employer to setup

---

[2] www.insurance.com. *Understanding the diffierence between HMO, PPO and POS.* Retrieved August 4, 2007, from http://www.insurance.com/Article.aspx/HMO,_PPO_and_POS_Health_Plans/artid/70

the reimbursement account than to pay the higher premiums of other plans. Some companies reimburse the full amount of the in-network deductible to encourage their employees to select the HRA plan over other plans. Since most employees won't incur large medical expenses during the year, the company saves significant money even while offering full reimbursement of the in-network deductible. (For a better understanding of HRA plans and their financial impact, visit: *http://www.ebri.org/pdf/ publications/testimony/t140.pdf*)

7.2.2 Retirement Plans

Retirement plans??? Yes, retirement plans. You need to start thinking about planning for retirement now, no matter how young you are. In fact, the younger you start planning, the better shape you will be in. Start planning in your early twenties and you could be a millionaire by the time you retire. Wait until you are in your thirties and you may be able to save several hundred thousands of dollars. Wait until you are in your forties and you will have substantially less savings. The point is, it is never too early to start planning for the future. In fact, not planning could mean financial disaster for you in the future.

There are two types of retirement plan categories available to you through your employer.[3] (This section will only cover employee-sponsored retirement accounts.

1. **Defined benefit plans.** Employer-sponsored pension plans guarantee a certain level of income after retirement. The amount you receive is usually based upon the number of years you have worked and provides you with a percentage of the average salary you were earning the final three to five years of your employment. For example, after completing twenty-five years of employment, you can retire with 50 percent pay for the remainder of your life. Often these benefits will also extend to your spouse. Most companies today are moving away from pension plans and are offering defined contribution plans. However, pensions are still offered by many union-based industries, some corporations, government jobs, and public schools.

2. **Defined contribution plans.** Most employers today are choosing to offer defined contribution plans over defined benefit plans. These plans center on individual accounts which often both the employer and the employee can contribute to. Income is not

---

[3] *Pension.* July, 2007. Retrieved August 4, 2007, from http://en.wikipedia.org/wiki/Defined_benefit_plan#Types_of_pensions

guaranteed and the actual value of the account will depend on the amount contributed and how the money is invested. There are several types of defined contribution plans that your employer has the option to offer.

FINANCIAL TIP

Always take advantage of any corporate sponsored retirement accounts that provide a match. It is free money in your pocket above your salary.

- **401(k) plan.** This is one of the more common types of retirement plans offered by an employer. In this plan, the employee contributes a tax deductible percentage of his or her salary into the account. Often the employer will match your contribution at a certain percentage. For example, if you make $50,000 per year and contribute 10 percent of your salary to the 401(k) plan you would only pay income taxes on $45,000. $5,000 would go into the 401(k) account to be invested and saved for retirement. Additionally, your employer may provide a match of your funds contributed. The amount your employer will match varies by company policy, but for the above example let's assume the employer matches your contributions at 50 percent up to 10 percent of your salary. That means if you contribute 10 percent or $5,000, the employer will contribute $2,500. You just made a 50 percent return on your money or received a $2,500 bonus on top of your salary. This money will now grow if invested properly and you will not have to pay taxes on the income until you retire and start to withdraw the money.

So why is your employer being so generous? It is simple. They want good employees to stay with the company. When you make contributions to the 401(k) account, your money is always your money, but to get the full amount of the employer's match you must stay with the company for a certain number of years. This is called vesting. Each year you are employed with the company, it vests you at a larger percentage. Many companies require you to stay with the company for five years to be 100 percent vested. They give you 20 percent per year until you reach the full five years. For example, if you leave the company after working there three years, you will leave with 100 percent of the money you contributed and 60 percent of your employer's matching contributions.

HOW MUCH WILL MY 401(K) BE WORTH?

To project how much your 401(k) account may be worth, check out the 401(k) calculator at: http://www.finance.cch.com/sohoApplets/Retire401k.asp

401(k) facts

- **Contribution limits for 2007.** $15,500 if you are under age 50. If you are over 50, you can contribute an additional $5,000 catch-up contribution.

- **Protection.** Your 401(k) plan is protected even if your company goes out of business. Your employer does not own your 401(k) account. It is an account that is kept in trust for you.

- **Take it with you.** If you leave your job, you can transfer your 401(k) balance to your new employer's 401(k) plan. You also have the option to rollover your 401(k) account into a traditional IRA.

- **Withdrawals.** Once you reach the age of 59 1/2 you can start withdrawing your money without incurring a penalty. You are still required to pay income taxes on your withdrawals, but if you are retired, you are probably in a lower tax bracket than when you were employed. If you withdraw the money before age 59 1/2 , you will incur a 10 percent federal tax penalty in addition to the income tax on your withdrawal. (There are certain hardship exceptions to the 10 percent penalty.) You must start taking withdrawals by age 70 1/2 unless you are still employed full-time with the sponsoring company of the 401(k) plan. In this case, you can defer this mandatory withdrawal.

- **Take a loan.** Although it is not recommended, you may take a loan from your 401(k) and make payments back into your account. You may borrow up to half the value of your account and have five years to pay back the money. (If you leave your job you must pay the money back within thirty days.) This is not a good idea, because the growth of your money will only be at the low interest rate you are paying yourself. Additionally, you are paying back the loan with after-tax dollars, when you borrowed your own pretax dollars. This more than offsets any interest you are paying back to your 401(k). (If you have the ability to take a loan as a mortgage or a home equity loan, the interest payment is tax deductible.)

- **403(b) plan.** This retirement plan is similar to the 401(k) plan except it is only available to nonprofit organizations including colleges, hospitals, public schools, and other nonprofit corporations.

- **457 plan.** Also a similar setup to the 401(k) plan, the 457 plan is offered by state and local government agencies.[4]

- **SEP-IRA (simplified employee pension plan).** Most IRAs are self-sponsored retirement accounts; however, the SEP-IRA is a simple plan that only your employer can contribute to. It is simple to set up, so it is ideal for a small business. Employees are always 100 percent vested and would have similar investment options as the 401(k) plan. For more information on SEP-IRAs, visit: http:// www.irs.gov/retirement/sponsor/article/0,,id=13 9828,00.html.

- **Profit sharing plan.** Either part of your 401(k) plan or as a separate benefit, your employer can provide a profit sharing plan of up to 25 percent of your salary based upon the company's performance.

7.2.3 Dental and Vision Insurance

Many companies provide dental and vision insurance in addition to health insurance. These plans usually operate like an HMO or PPO except they specialize in either dental or vision. Although these are great benefits to have, their coverage is usually limited as far as their annual payouts. For example, your dental plan may cover you for checkups and cleaning. However, they may cap their annual payout to $2,000 per year per person. Vision would have similar coverage with an annual cap of about $250 per year or a new pair of glasses every two years.

7.2.4 Short-Term Disability and Long-Term Disability Insurance

Short-term disability insurance will protect you in the event you become ill or disabled for a period that extends past your number of sick days up to a term of one year, depending on your policy. The coverage will usually pay you between 50 percent and 66 2/3 percent of your salary or a predefined dollar amount. State benefits and private benefits will vary

---

[4] IRS. *IRC 457(b) Deferred Compensation Plans.* Retrieved November 2, 2006, from http:// www.irs.gov/retirement/article/0,,id=111442,00.html

depending on job location and the private policy your company has. Additionally, the cost will vary. Some employers pay the entire premium, while other employers will have the employee pay some or the entire premium.

Long-term disability insurance will help replace lost wages up to age 65 if you become disabled. Coverage will usually start after your short-term disability insurance ends or after one year of being disabled. The coverage generally pays you between 50 percent and 66 2/3 percent of your salary or a predefined dollar amount. When your employer pays for the benefit and you ever have to make a claim, your benefits will be considered taxable income to you. However, if you elect to pay the premium, your benefits are tax free and will more likely cover your living expenses. In actuality 66 2/3 percent of your wages tax free is much closer to your take home pay amount than having that payment taxed.

7.2.5 Stock Purchasing Plans and Stock Options

Many publicly traded companies will allow employees the opportunity to divert a percentage of their wages into an investment account and purchase company stock at a discount. For example, the stock purchasing plan may allow you to contribute up to 10 percent of your salary into the account and purchase stock quarterly at a 15 percent discount off the lowest price of the quarter. In a well-performing company, this can be a very lucrative benefit. However, be cautious; there is risk involved anytime you invest in stocks.

An employee stock option plan gives the employee the option to purchase a certain number of shares at a predefined price. For example, at the time of employment, the stock might be at $8 per share. You are then given an option to buy 500 shares at a price of $8 per share. If the stock goes up, you can exercise the option at a later date and make an instant profit.[5]

7.2.6 Vacation Days, Sick Days, and Personal Days

Part of your compensation package should include paid vacation, sick, and personal days. A typical package will include something approximating ten vacation days, five sick days, and two personal days.

7.3 ACCEPTING THE JOB

Congratulations! You have successfully negotiated a job offer. Before giving notice at your current job that you are leaving, make sure your new

---

[5] SEC. *Employee Stock Option Plans*. Retrieved November 2, 2006, from http://www.sec.gov/answers/empopt.htm

employer gives you an offer letter. The letter should state your job title, start date, salary, supervisor, vacation days, sick days, personal days, and benefits. Additionally, they should also provide you with a job description which outlines your responsibilities.

To demonstrate your professionalism and to confirm your acceptance of the position, you should send your new employer a letter of acceptance. Your letter should also highlight the terms of your agreement. Make sure to include your position title, salary, benefits overview, and start date.

Sample Acceptance Letter (Figure 7–1)

Andrew Jones
1644 Broadway · New York, NY 10019 · 708.555.5555 ·
e-mail: Andy_Jones@Careercrib.com

May 03, 20XX

Jocelyn Jennings
Retro Gaming Unlimited
1223 5th Avenue
New York, NY 10014

Dear Ms. Jocelyn Jennings:

It is with great pleasure and anticipation that I accept your offer to join your team as the Assistant Game Artist. As we discussed, I will be starting a week from Monday at a salary of $32,000 per year. My health benefits are scheduled to start on June 1st and I will be eligible to join the 401(k) plan after one year of employment.

Thank you for the time you spent with me during the interview process. The job description you provided me with has given me a solid understanding of what is expected of me. I look forward to the challenges that lie ahead. I want to thank you for this opportunity and I look forward to working for you.

If there is any paperwork or other information I can provide you with prior to my start date, please let me know.

Sincerely,

Andrew Jones

Andrew Jones

FIGURE 7-1   Acceptance letter

7.4 ADAPTING TO YOUR WORK ENVIRONMENT

Your first day on the new job can often be challenging. Learning to adapt to your new working environment can be tricky if you do not know how to approach it. The first thing you should do is familiarize yourself with company policies. Most of these policies are listed in the employee handbook. You should read the handbook prior to your first day on the job.

Secondly, dress appropriately for the job. After interviewing, you should be familiar with the dress code of the company. You are better off being a little overdressed the first day than being underdressed. Also make sure to introduce yourself to your new co-workers. Be friendly and courteous to everybody you meet.

Do not be afraid to ask questions. Many people are afraid to look like they do not know what they are doing, but your employer expects there to be a learning curve for you. When you are unsure of something, ask. Be up front with your employer about what you know and do not know. If you need additional training, take it upon yourself to learn the skill necessary for your position.

Every office has its own culture. Some working environments are more competitive than others. As long as you mind your own business and do not get caught up in company gossip you will be successful. You never know who knows who outside of the office or who will be promoted next and could be your next supervisor. As long as you are a productive employee and continue to be a positive influence in the office, you will be successful.

7.5 REJECTING A JOB OFFER

Not all job offers will be a good match for you. When offered a position, the job must be a position that you can see yourself in for a while. Is the compensation and benefits package something you can live with? Do the hours work for you? Is the commute reasonable? How is the working environment? Does your supervisor seem like somebody who you will like working for? These are all things to consider when offered a position.

If you decide to reject a job offer, you still must be professional in your approach. You do not want to burn your bridges at the company you are rejecting. You may choose to reapply for a position at the company in the future. It is also possible that you will run into the same supervisor at another company in the future. Just because you rejected an offer before does not mean that they will never consider you for a future position. When rejecting an offer, write a professional letter and send it in a timely matter.

Sample Job Rejection Letter (Figure 7–2)

Andrew Jones
1644 Broadway · New York, NY 10019 · 708.555.5555 ·
e-mail: Andy_Jones@Careercrib.com

May 03, 20XX

Jocelyn Jennings
Retro Gaming Unlimited
1223 5th Avenue
New York, NY 10014

Dear Ms. Jocelyn Jennings:

I would like to thank you for offering me the position of Assistant Game Artist. I greatly appreciate the consideration for the position; however I have chosen to accept an offer with another company. This was a very difficult decision, but the other position was a better match for my goals at this time.

I would like to extend my gratitude to your team for the time they spent with me. The current projects they described to me are very exciting and I hope we have the opportunity to work together in some other capacity in the future.

Thank you again for your consideration. I wish your company success in the future and I hope our professional paths cross again.

Sincerely,

Andrew Jones

Andrew Jones

FIGURE 7-2   Job rejection letter

REVIEW QUESTIONS/ACTIVITIES

Research Salaries in Your Area

- Break up into small groups and research entry-level salaries for various in-field positions in your geographical area. Also research the type of benefits package usually offered.

Salary and Benefits Self-Analysis

- Create a list outlining your minimum requirements for accepting a job offer. List your salary range and benefits necessary.

1. List three different types of health insurance plans. List out the advantages and disadvantages of each plan.

2. What is the difference between a "defined benefits plan" and a "defined contribution plan"?

3. What is "vesting"? Give an example of a vesting schedule.

4. List at least five important items to consider when evaluating a job offer.

5. Draft a sample job acceptance letter. What major points should it cover?

Working Freelance

OUTLINE

OBJECTIVES

- Learn how to start freelancing
- Learn how to legally start your own business
- Learn how to promote yourself
- Learn how to establish relationships with clients
- Learn how to create a start-up budget
- Learn how to price your services
- Learn how to create multiple profit centers

INTRODUCTION

Working as a freelancer in the media fields can be a rewarding experience both financially and personally. Many media designers work full-time and freelance on the side or create a career based strictly on freelancing. There are many advantages to freelancing. It allows you to choose your clients, create your own work schedule, and keep all the profits for yourself. However, it also creates many challenges; you need to find clients, expand your work schedule, and make a profit. You will also need to form a start-up budget, purchase equipment, create marketing material, prepare your portfolio, learn how to keep accounting books, find time to network with clients, and face all the challenges of owning a small business.

Sound intimidating? It can be, but it can also be very rewarding. If you are still in school, this is the perfect opportunity to start freelancing. You have access to equipment and you have your professors as a resource that may be able to help you with your designing and technical needs. This is also a good opportunity to start building a portfolio of freelance projects. Few potential clients will hire a freelance designer without seeing a portfolio of professional work. Therefore, you need to work on as many projects as possible. Start out by volunteering your services for a local charity. Approach your friends and family who own their own businesses and ask if you can redesign some business cards, letterheads, marketing material, or their website. Volunteer your services to create a promotional video. Do whatever you can to start designing.

You can start small with just a few clients and the drive to succeed. You do not need to make a huge investment to start testing the market and see if freelancing is for you. However, at a certain point, when you decide that you want to make a career out of freelancing, you will obviously need to invest money in your new venture. Your start-up might be as simple as converting a room in your home into an office, and purchasing a new computer, software, and whatever other equipment you will need to start working (i.e., scanners, printers, cameras, etc.). Another option is to rent certain equipment as you need it per job. For example, if you are shooting a thirty second commercial for a client, you don't need to own all of the video or film equipment. You can either rent out a production studio for the day or rent the needed equipment for an on-location shoot. Make sure to bill the client for the time and the equipment.

8.1 STARTING YOUR OWN BUSINESS

Anybody can start his or her own business. You just need a business plan. One of the biggest mistakes people make when starting a business is not having a written plan. You need to take the time and put your idea in writing. There are many free Internet sources for sample business plans. Visit:

- *http://sbdcnet.org/SBIC/bplans.php*
- *http://www.businessplanarchive.org*
- *http://www.bplans.com/samples/mbus.cfm*
- *http://www.entrepreneur.com/businessplan/index.html*

8.1.1 Writing the Plan

(Excerpt from: *Write a Business Plan.* U.S. Small Business Administration, http://www.sba.gov/smallbusinessplanner/plan/writeabusinessplan/SERV_WRRITINGBUSPLAN.html)

What goes in a business plan? The body can be divided into four distinct sections:

1. Description of the business
2. Marketing
3. Finances
4. Management

The agenda should include an executive summary, supporting documents, and financial projections. Although there is no single formula for developing a business plan, some elements are common to all business plans. They are summarized in the following outline:

Elements of a business plan
1. Cover sheet
2. Statement of purpose
3. Table of contents
I. The Business
   A. Description of business
   B. Marketing
   C. Competition
   D. Operating procedures
   E. Personnel
   F. Business insurance
II. Financial Data
   A. Loan applications
   B. Capital equipment and supply list
   C. Balance sheet

D. Break-even analysis

E. Pro-forma income projections (profit and loss statements)

F. Three-year summary

G. Detail by month, first year

H. Detail by quarters, second and third years

I. Assumptions upon which projections were based

J. Pro-forma cash flow

III. Supporting Documents

A. Tax returns of principals for last three years; personal financial statement (all banks have these forms)

B. For franchised businesses, a copy of franchise contract and all supporting documents provided by the franchisor

C. Copy of proposed lease or purchase agreement for building space

D. Copy of licenses and other legal documents

E. Copy of resumes of all principals

F. Copies of letters of intent from suppliers, and so on.

8.2 LEGAL WAYS TO STRUCTURE YOUR BUSINESS

(When deciding which type of business structure to choose, it is best to consult professional legal advice.)

There are several legal options when starting your own business. Each legal option will have different tax and legal advantages and disadvantages. The type of option you choose will vary depending on what your goals are. According to the U.S. Small Business Administration (SBA—*www.sba. gov*) the five most common forms of business structures are:

- Sole proprietorships
- Partnerships
- Corporations
- Subchapter S corporations
- Limited liability company (LLC)

(The following is an overview of several options provided by the SBA—U.S. Small Business Association. Source: http://www.sba.gov/smallbusinessplanner/start/chooseastructure/ START_FORMS_OWNERSHIP.html)

Consider the following questions when choosing a business structure:

- Your vision regarding the size and nature of your business.
- The level of control you wish to have.

- The level of structure you are willing to deal with.
- The business's vulnerability to lawsuits.
- Tax implications of the different ownership structures.
- Expected profit (or loss) of the business.
- Whether or not you need to reinvest earnings into the business.
- Your need for access to cash out of the business for yourself.

8.2.1 Sole Proprietorships

The vast majority of small businesses start out as sole proprietorships. These firms are owned by one person, usually the individual who has day-to-day responsibilities for running the business. Sole proprietors own all the assets of the business and the profits generated by it. They also assume complete responsibility for any of its liabilities or debts. In the eyes of the law and the public, you are one in the same with the business.

Advantages of a sole proprietorship
- It is the easiest and least expensive form of ownership to organize.
- Sole proprietors are in complete control and, within the parameters of the law, may make decisions as they see fit.
- Sole proprietors receive all income generated by the business to keep or reinvest.
- Profits from the business flow directly to the owner's personal tax return.
- The business is easy to dissolve, if desired.

Disadvantages of a sole proprietorship
- Sole proprietors have unlimited liability and are legally responsible for all debts against the business. Their business and personal assets are at risk.
- They may be at a disadvantage in raising funds and are often limited to using funds from personal savings or consumer loans.
- They may have a hard time attracting high-caliber employees or those that are motivated by the opportunity to own a part of the business.
- Some employee benefits such as owner's medical insurance premiums are not directly deductible from business income (only partially deductible as an adjustment to income).

Federal tax forms for sole proprietorship (only a partial list and some may not apply)
- Form 1040: Individual Income Tax Return
- Schedule C: Profit or Loss from Business (or Schedule C-EZ)
- Schedule SE: Self-Employment Tax
- Form 1040-ES: Estimated Tax for Individuals
- Form 4562: Depreciation and Amortization
- Form 8829: Expenses for Business Use of Your Home
- Employment Tax Forms

8.2.2 Partnerships

In a partnership, two or more people share ownership of a single business. Like proprietorships, the law does not distinguish between the business and its owners. The partners should have a legal agreement that sets forth how decisions will be made, profits will be shared, disputes will be resolved, how future partners will be admitted to the partnership, how partners can be bought out, and what steps will be taken to dissolve the partnership when needed. Yes, it's hard to think about a breakup when the business is just getting started, but many partnerships split up at crisis times, and unless there is a defined dissolution process, there will be even greater problems. Partners also must decide up-front how much time and capital each will contribute, and so on.

Advantages of a partnership
- Partnerships are relatively easy to establish; however, time should be invested in developing the partnership agreement.
- With more than one owner, the ability to raise funds may be increased.
- The profits from the business flow directly through to the partners' personal tax returns.
- Prospective employees may be attracted to the business if given the incentive to become a partner.
- The business usually will benefit from partners who have complementary skills.

Disadvantages of a partnership
- Partners are jointly and individually liable for the actions of the other partners.
- Profits must be shared with others.
- Since decisions are shared, disagreements can occur.

- Some employee benefits are not deductible from business income on tax returns.
- The partnership may have a limited life; it may end upon the withdrawal or death of a partner.

Types of partnerships that should be considered:
1. **General partnership.** Partners divide responsibility for management and liability as well as the shares of profit or loss according to their internal agreement. Equal shares are assumed unless there is a written agreement that states differently.
2. **Limited partnership and partnership with limited liability.** Limited means that most of the partners have limited liability (to the extent of their investment) as well as limited input regarding management decisions, which generally encourages investors for short-term projects or for investing in capital assets. This form of ownership is not often used for operating retail or service businesses. Forming a limited partnership is more complex and formal than that of a general partnership.
3. **Joint venture.** Acts like a general partnership, but is clearly for a limited period of time or a single project. If the partners in a joint venture repeat the activity, they will be recognized as an ongoing partnership and will have to file as such as well as distribute accumulated partnership assets upon dissolution of the entity.

Federal tax forms for partnerships (only a partial list and some may not apply)
- Form 1065: Partnership Return of Income
- Form 1065 K-1: Partner's Share of Income, Credit, Deductions
- Form 4562: Depreciation
- Form 1040: Individual Income Tax Return
- Schedule E: Supplemental Income and Loss
- Schedule SE: Self-Employment Tax
- Form 1040-ES: Estimated Tax for Individuals
- Employment Tax Forms

8.2.3 Corporations

A corporation chartered by the state in which it is headquartered is considered by law to be a unique entity, separate and apart from those who own it. A corporation can be taxed, it can be sued, and it can enter into contractual agreements. The owners of a corporation are its shareholders. The shareholders elect a board of directors to oversee the major policies and decisions. The corporation has a life of its own and does not dissolve when ownership changes.

Advantages of a corporation
- Shareholders have limited liability for the corporation's debts or judgments against the corporation.
- Generally, shareholders can only be held accountable for their investment in stock of the company. (Note, however, that officers can be held personally liable for their actions, such as the failure to withhold and pay employment taxes.)
- Corporations can raise additional funds through the sale of stock.
- A corporation may deduct the cost of benefits it provides to officers and employees.
- A corporation can elect S corporation status if certain requirements are met. This election enables the company to be taxed similar to a partnership.

Disadvantages of a corporation
- The process of incorporation requires more time and money than other forms of organization.
- Corporations are monitored by federal, state, and some local agencies, and as a result may have more paperwork to comply with regulations.
- Incorporating may result in higher overall taxes. Dividends paid to shareholders are not deductible from business income; thus, it can be taxed twice.

Federal tax forms for regular or "C" corporations (only a partial list and some may not apply)
- Form 1120 or 1120-A: Corporation Income Tax Return
- Form 1120-W: Estimated Tax for Corporation
- Form 8109-B: Deposit Coupon
- Form 4625: Depreciation
- Employment Tax Forms
- Other forms as needed for capital gains, sale of assets, alternative minimum tax, and so on.

8.2.4 Subchapter S Corporations

A tax election only; this election enables the shareholder to treat the earnings and profits as distributions and have them pass through directly to their personal tax return. The catch here is that the share-holder, if working for the company, must pay him/herself wages if there is a profit, and must meet standards of "reasonable compensation." This can vary by geographical region as well as occupation, but the basic rule is to pay yourself what you would have to pay someone to do your job, as long as there is enough profit. If you do not do this, the IRS can reclassify all of the earnings and profit as wages, and you will be liable for all of the payroll taxes on the total amount.

Federal tax forms for subchapter S corporations (only a partial list and some may not apply)

- Form 1120S: Income Tax Return for S Corporation
- 1120S K-1: Shareholder's Share of Income, Credit, Deductions
- Form 4625: Depreciation
- Employment Tax Forms
- Form 1040: Individual Income Tax Return
- Schedule E: Supplemental Income and Loss
- Schedule SE: Self-Employment Tax
- Form 1040-ES: Estimated Tax for Individuals
- Other forms as needed for capital gains, sale of assets, alternative minimum tax, and so on.

8.2.5 Limited Liability Company (LLC)

The LLC is a relatively new type of hybrid business structure that is now permissible in most states. It is designed to provide the limited liability features of a corporation and the tax efficiencies and operational flexibility of a partnership. Formation is more complex and formal than that of a general partnership.

The owners are members, and the duration of the LLC is usually determined when the organization papers are filed. The time limit can be continued, if desired, by a vote of the members at the time of expiration. LLCs must not have more than two of the four characteristics that define corporations: limited liability to the extent of assets, continuity of life, centralization of management, and free transferability of ownership interests.

8.2.6 DBA (Doing Business As)

If you decide not to incorporate, but still want to use another name other than your own to conduct business, you should file a DBA form with your local county clerk's office. A DBA will allow you to conduct business and open a bank account under the assumed name. Remember, a DBA does not offer you any of the protections of incorporating.

It is strictly a legal notification that you will be conducting your business under name other than your legal birth name. If you need liability protection, it is best to consult a legal professional and explore which business structure is right for you.

The cost of filing a DBA will vary from state to state and sometimes will also vary depending on the county you want to file in. The cost can range from $5.00 (Connecticut) to $195.00 (several counties in California). In most counties, the cost is less than $50.00. To find out what your county charges, contact your local county clerk's office.

Filling out the form is relatively easy and you probably can do it yourself. Usually the county clerk's office is more than willing to assist you in filling out your form. Additionally, the clerk's office will do a free search for you to see if anybody else is conducting business under the name you would like to use. The information you will need to fill out the form will vary state to state, but will most likely include the following information:

- Your name
- Home address
- Address where you will be conducting business
- Name which you will be conducting business under

There may be different forms depending on whether you are filing a DBA as an individual, partnership, or corporation. Make sure you are using the correct form.

8.3 MARKETING AND SELF-PROMOTION

Marketing and promoting your new business venture is very important. You are not going to get any business without potential clients knowing you exist. There are several methods to self-promotion and you should use all of them.

8.3.1 Marketing Material

1. **Business card.** You need a business card! Every time you meet somebody, hand out your business card. Remember that your business card is your strongest marketing piece. You can be creative in the design, but keep your card simple to read and make sure it is easy to find your information. Your card should include your:

   a. Name

   b. Company name or title of what you do (if applicable)

   c. Phone number

d. Address

e. E-mail

f. Website URL

g. A brief description of your services. For example, if you are a graphic designer, you might list out the type of projects you specialize in (i.e., logo and brand identity, website design, letterheads and business cards, etc.)

WEBSITE NAVIGATION

Make sure your website's navigation is simple and consistent. Once a user becomes familiar with your website setup, do not significantly change the way a user gets to the next Web page. A frustrated user will just go to the next website that is easier to navigate.

2. **Website.** Every freelancer needs a website. It is a great marketing tool in which you can point potential clients to view your portfolio, find out about your services, and contact you. The design of your website is a big piece of your image and professionalism. Make sure your site is professional and easy to navigate. Choose your design theme carefully. Remember who your target market is and design your site with your clients in mind. If you produce music videos, your website should have a completely different look than that of a children's book illustrator. Your site should include:

a. **Homepage.** Your homepage should let the viewer know right away what you do. Your navigation on the homepage should be easy to use and find. Keep your navigation consistent throughout the site.

b. **Portfolio.** Include samples of your work. This is the first thing your client is going to review when considering hiring you. If you are not a Web designer and need to hire someone to design your site, this is where you should put your money.

c. **List of former clients and client testimonials.** Potential clients want to know who you have worked for. If you are new to the business and do not have clients to list, start keeping track now and create this page once you have a list of eight to twelve professional clients. If your former clients have websites, you may wish to include links to their sites. It is also a good idea to request that your clients write you a brief testimonial upon completion of their project. Satisfied former clients are your best marketing tool.

d. **About you.** A description of your services and biography of you or your company will give potential clients an image to attach to your company name. Again, keep it professional and focus it on your target client.

e. **Contact you.** An e-mail form is a much better way of contacting you than just your e-mail address as a link. This will ensure that your e-mail is sent to you and it also allows you to request important information such as the phone number and full name of the person submitting the contact request. It will also help you cut down on spam mail. In addition, you may wish to include your business telephone number and address (if you work from home, you might just want to put your city and state without your street address to inform clients of your geographical location).

3. **Postcards.** Creating a marketing postcard is a simple, inexpensive way to keep in touch with current and potential clients. It keeps your company name fresh in their heads and allows you to send reminders, announcements of new services, coupons for services such as printing, or anything else you would like to communicate. Your postcard will also serve as a design sample. Print at least one side in full color and use that space for your visual presentation of your work and perhaps a line or two of marketing headlines. The second side should include a written message with updates about your services or information you are conveying. Remember to include your contact information and website on the postcard.

4. **Portfolio/demo reel.** You already have a portfolio or demo reel to present at a meeting. You should also create a version that you can mail or leave with potential clients. Formats can include:

a. **Digital portfolio.** Create a CD-ROM/DVD-ROM of your portfolio or demo reel. Remember to package it professionally. This includes creating a printed label for the disc, a traycard, and an insert cover. If your packaging looks enticing, clients are more likely to view your portfolio versus a CD-ROM with your name written on it with a permanent marker.

b. **Bound booklet.** Creating full-color booklets is more expensive, but makes a great impression. This is especially true if you are targeting higher end clients. Make sure to include a list of your services within the booklet.

c. **Pamphlets.** Marketing pamphlets can include both samples of your portfolio and a list of your services.

5. **Promotional video.** Depending on your services and budget, you may consider creating a promotional video. This is especially a good idea if you are in the business of promotional videos. Let the client see what they can expect from your services. In addition to

distributing your video on DVD, you can also stream your video over your website.

6. **Promotional signs.** If your place of business is in a commercial location, a sign in front of your office is a great way to promote your business. Home office-based businesses may have a problem placing signs on your front lawn. You need to check with your local town to see if it is in violation of town zoning laws before you place an advertisement in front of your house or apartment. Some towns will allow you to hang a shingle like a doctor's office. This may be an option for your home-based business.

8.3.2 Networking

Your best marketing tool is yourself. Nothing will help establish and maintain your business better than your own ability to network. Networking requires that you are always self-promoting. It is all about making connections, both professional and personal. You should always be prepared to discuss your services, your latest project, and your level of customer service. Always carry your business card with you. You should hand it to everybody you meet that may need your services in the future.

There are many places to network. Industry organizations such as the Graphic Artist Guild, NATPE (National Association of Television Program Executives), AES (Audio Engineering Society), and NAB (National Association of Broadcasters) are all great places to network. Most organizations have local chapters with regular meetings and often host networking events. Additionally, many of these organizations host annual conventions where vendors set up booths to demonstrate the latest technology and host training seminars. Attending these annual conventions is a must for any industry professional and is the perfect opportunity to network.

In addition to attending networking events that are focused on your profession, it is also a good idea to attend networking events for industries that may need your services. For example, a photographer should attend events for the NPPA (National Press Photographers Association), and should also attend events for magazine and newspaper publishers, wedding services, and art gallery events to network with potential clients, not just other members of the photography profession.

8.3.3 Start a Networking Database

Keep a database of your networking contacts. Your database should include:

- Company name
- Contact name

- Telephone number
- Address
- E-mail
- Website
- Description of company
- Contact log

Use this database to keep track of everybody you meet. Send regular updates about your services to your network using multiple mediums to contact them. Alternate your contact methods between e-mails, postcard and letter mailings, telephone calls, and visiting them in person when appropriate. The key to successful networking is maintaining a personal connection with the client. You may wish to create a monthly newsletter and include articles that address areas your network would be interested in reading. Keep them looking forward to your newsletter. Perhaps you can allow your network to contribute to your newsletter. The key is doing whatever it takes to keep your name in the minds of potential clients.

8.3.4 Word of Mouth

KEEP A PORTFOLIO OF SATISFIED CLIENTS

Ask satisfied clients to write a letter to you expressing their satisfaction. Keep these letters in a high quality portfolio, binder, or album and keep it available for new clients to see. If possible, layout the thank-you letters in a portfolio with a copy of the work you created for them. This can include sample print products, screen shots, photographs, or any other visual representation you can place in a print portfolio.

Your best source of business is your reputation. No piece of marketing material can get you business like a satisfied client spreading the word about your great services. Although it takes time to build a reputation, there are things you can do to help this process along.

1. **Make sure your clients are satisfied with your product.** This is one of the most important things you can do to build a strong reputation. A little extra effort on your part will go a long way in establishing your reputation for delivering a quality product. If this means putting in a few extra hours without getting paid or throwing in a little something extra into a package, do it. Clients always like to feel that they received a good deal.

2. **Charge a fair price.** Do not nickel and dime clients to get every cent you can bill out of them. You may make a few extra dollars

on the current job, but clients are more likely to come back to you if they feel like you treated them fairly and did not squeeze them. This does not mean you work for free; it just means you are a little flexible and round in the client's favor occasionally.

3. **Deliver on time.** Bottom line, you need to meet your deadlines. Clients will pay a premium if they know you will meet their deadlines and deliver a quality product. As your reputation builds for being reliable, your ability to charge more will increase. Nothing is more important than a dependable vendor, especially when there is an important job.

4. **Become an industry expert!** You want to be the "go-to" person whenever there is a technical or industry question. If clients know they can call you for some quick advice, your reputation will grow and you will be known as the "go-to" person for answers. As clients depend upon you for answers, your name will spread rapidly as clients share your name with other industry professionals who also need answers.

5. **Be easy to work with.** Clients like to work with vendors who are easy to work with. Maintain a positive attitude and deliver what your client asks for. Do not argue with your clients. You may make professional and creative suggestions, but the bottom line is the clients are paying you and you must do what they are asking.

6. **Show you care.** Show enthusiasm for the project. Never let a freelance job just be another paycheck to you. The project is important to your client and should be equally important to you. Demonstrate to the client that you are also vested in the success of their business and you will help build a positive long-term relationship.

7. **Provide a high level of customer service.** Make sure you back your product. If any issues arise after the project is finished, continue to service your product. There are limits to this, but standing behind your product demonstrates that your clients are important to you and shows your dependability. The bottom line is clients will come back to you when they know you will take care of them as issues arise.

8.4 HOW MUCH TO CHARGE FOR FREELANCE WORK

One of the most challenging issues facing freelancers is how much to charge. Your rates for projects will vary greatly depending on your geographical area, experience, the scope of the project, type of client, and local competition. When setting your rate you must think beyond just the amount of money you want for your time. Factors to consider in setting your rate include:

- **Hourly rate you want for yourself.** This includes both time you can bill for and time needed that is not billable. For example, you may need to conduct research or travel for the job. This needs to be accounted for in your rate.

  - Your expenses and overhead for operating your own business:
  - Office supplies
  - Maintenance of your equipment
  - Software
  - Reference books
  - Media for backing up your work
  - Advertising and marketing expenses
  - Taxes related to being self-employed
  - Providing your own benefits (if you do not have another job that provides you with benefits)
  - Insurance
  - Legal fees

    (These are just a few of the expenses that you will be responsible for and must consider when setting your price.)

- **Your competition.** What your competition is charging for similar work will impact your ability to charge a higher rate. This will vary greatly depending on your geographical area. You may want to conduct some local research and call some local companies to find out what they are charging for similar services.

- **How established you are in the field.** Over time, you will be able to increase your rates as you develop a reputation. This may mean that you cannot charge what you like when you are establishing yourself, but this will change as your reputation grows in the industry.

- **Target market.** Who are the clients that you are targeting? The type of client you seek out will affect your rates. Large corporations will often have larger budgets to work with than your average Mom and Pop shop. However, it may be easier to network with the smaller companies. Many large companies will prefer to work with other large established companies.

- **Profit.** You do not just want to break even on the work you are completing. You want your freelance business to generate a profit beyond covering your hourly rate and expenses. One effective strategy to increasing your revenue is to create multiple profit centers.

8.4.1 Creating Multiple Profit Centers

An effective method to generating additional revenue for your business is to offer multiple services. For example, if you design a brochure for a company, do not just offer your design services; provide printing services as well. This does not mean that you are going to print the brochures yourself. You will subcontract the printing job to another vendor.

As a freelancer, you should establish working relationships with companies that offer related services to your services. Create a list of vendors such as printing, Web hosting, CD/DVD duplication, computer and software distributors, or anything else related to your services. Contact these companies and ask for discounted prices or wholesale prices. Many of these companies will provide you better pricing or a commission for referrals because you will be able to provide them consistent business. The discounted prices will give you a margin to mark up the services and resell them to your clients. In many cases, you will make a larger profit on the additional services you offer than just your hourly or packaged rate for designing something.

This is a standard and ethical practice. In fact, you may get additional jobs because you offer additional services. A client wants to go to one place for all of their needs. They will often pay a premium for these services for the convenience, customer service, and dependability of working only with you. Make sure the vendors and subcontractors you are working with are reputable and will meet your deadlines. Your clients are not going to care why their jobs are not finished; it is still going to be your responsibility.

8.5 GET IT IN WRITING — DRAFTING A CONTRACT

(The information in this section is strictly for educational purposes and does not constitute legal advice. Always consult a legal professional when drafting and signing contracts.)

No matter who the client is, always have an agreement in writing. This is equally important when working with strangers or friends and family. Laying out your terms in writing will protect all parties involved, set out the expectations and guidelines for the project, and address unforeseen issues that may arise. It is highly recommended that you work with a legal professional to draft a contract. You can hire a legal professional to draft a standard contract that can be used for most of your freelance jobs.

Items and terms to include in your contract include, but are not limited to, the following:

- **List the parties involved.**   State the full names with addresses of all companies involved in the agreement. Also state the date of the contract.

- **Description of project.**   Give as much detail of the scope of the project as possible. The more defined the project is, the less room there is for misunderstandings or disputes upon delivery of the project. List what the project includes and list what is excluded. For example, when designing a website, include the number of Web pages and what type of technology will be used. When producing a promotional video, list the length of the video, how it will be delivered, and what is included and excluded such as the cost of talent, music, and licensed images.

- **Set the price and limits.**   Include the agreed-upon price. Also include provisions for the project growing beyond the description. This can be an hourly rate, a charge per additional item delivered, or any other term that is agreed upon. If you are completing the project as a flat fee, you need to set limits. For example, you are contracted to create a 3D animated logo for a flat price of $800. You need to set limits on the number of revisions and meetings that will be allowed and an hourly rate after the contracted number of revisions has been met. Include a clause such as, "All storyboards and sketches must be approved by _____. Upon approval, any additional changes to the storyboards will be charged at $80/hour. During the animation process, the animator will meet with the client two times for progress updates. Any additional meetings or additional revisions beyond the two meetings will be billed at $80/hour. There is a one hour minimum charge for all billable hours." Without such a clause, a client will be able to keep making changes for an extended period of time without paying you additional money.

- Payment terms.   List and define your payment terms. The following example represents possible payment terms for a website design:

- Payment terms:

  - One-Third of contract will be paid at time of contract.
  - One-Third will be paid within fifteen days of half completion.
    - Half completion is defined as new website design posted at *www.careercrib.com* with current HTML content only.
    - The database will not be operational at this stage.
    - Sections that include database technology will be posted as "Under Construction" or "Feature Coming Soon."

- Final One-Third paid within fifteen days of final completion.
- Completed website with functioning, searchable database.
- Any additional moneys owed are due within fifteen days of billing.
- Late payment fee is 1.5 percent per month.

- **Delivery date.** Include a timeframe of when the finished product will be delivered. You can include clauses such as, "The designer agrees to deliver the completed website within five weeks of Careercrib.com's acceptance of website page designs and flowchart."
- **Warranty and maintenance.** When designing websites, interactive presentations, or any other projects that may need routine maintenance, include a clause that outlines how long and what areas you will maintain. For example:
- **Warranty and Maintenance of Website:**
  - Upon final delivery, the designer agrees to maintain the website for a term of nine months to address technical issues and functionality of the website only. Any updates to the content within the website will be charged at $50 per Web page. Additional HTML Web page development will be billed at $80/hour. Additional charges for database or Web programming development will be agreed upon before inclusion within the website.
  - Website maintenance after the nine month warranty period will be billed at $200/month for technical and functionality issues. Content updates, if any, will be charged at $50 per page.
  - Either party may cancel the maintenance contract with sixty days notice after the nine month warranty period.
- **Reserve the right to demonstrate your work.** This may seem like a small thing, but make sure you put in a provision that allows you to show the work you produce to potential clients as part of your portfolio.
- **Kill fee.** Include a provision for the client canceling the project. For example, "If at any time Careercrib.com decides to cancel the design contract, a cancellation fee of all money currently paid, plus 50 percent of all additional money owed as stipulated in the contract for the completed project, must be paid. Minimum cancellation fee (kill fee) = $3,000. Upon cancellation, Careercrib.com forfeits all rights to use of any of the content created. The only exception to the kill fee is non-delivery of specified website as described within this agreement."

- **Permissions and using copyright protected material supplied by the company.** If the client is supplying you with content, make sure you include a clause that makes the client responsible for obtaining the proper rights to use the intellectual property of somebody else. For example, "Careercrib.com accepts all liability and is responsible for obtaining permissions for any material submitted to the designer."

- **Limit of liability.** Protect yourself against liability by including a clause that limits your liability to money that you have been paid by the client. For example, "Under no circumstance shall liability by the Designer exceed any moneys paid by Careercrib.com to the Designer, minus expenses incurred by the Designer."

- **Retain the rights to computer code.** When designing projects that include any type of computer code (i.e., HTML, PHP, Actionscript, ASP, Lingo, etc.), include a provision that allows you to reuse code in the future. This provision does not extend to front end design imagery, only to any code this is written. For example, "The designer and Web developers retain the right to reuse code at a later date."

REVIEW QUESTIONS/ACTIVITIES

Draft a business plan and start a fictitious business:

- Using the outline and reference links in this chapter, create an outline and draft a business plan for a business related to your course of study.

Create a marketing plan and marketing material for your new freelance business:

- Create and order business cards for yourself.
- Create promotional material such as postcards, brochures, and demo CD-ROMS/DVD-ROMS.
- Develop a website for your services. If you are a Web Designer, try to partner up with a person who is a Web Designer and offer to trade services.

Create a vendor database:

- Create a list of ten possible vendors whose services you can use as a freelancer. These vendors can include CD/DVD manufacturers,

Web hosting, equipment and supply companies, or another service you can use for your own business or resell to clients.

The database should include:

Name of company

Type of firm (what they specialize in)

Address

Phone number

Web address

Contact name (if possible)

CHAPTER 9

Protecting and Licensing Your Work

OUTLINE

OBJECTIVES

- Learn how to protect your intellectual property
- Learn how to file a copyright form
- Learn what form to use when filing a copyright
- Learn what is covered in a copyright
- Learn how to license your work
- Learn what constitutes fair use

The information in this chapter does not constitute legal advice. It is a guide to information. In cases needing legal advice, please consult the proper sources such as an attorney.

INTRODUCTION

As a person entering the design and media fields, it is important to understand how to protect your creative works. The idea of filing a copyright can seem to be a completely foreign concept at first, but is actually fairly easy to do. All that it requires is some basic information about the author or creator of the work, a copy of the work to file with the form, and a small fee.

9.1 WHAT IS A COPYRIGHT?

A **copyright** protects the owner of a creative work's legal rights to reproduce, distribute, publish, and sell their owned property. The work can either be published or unpublished. Copyright owners can also create derivative works based upon the original work, display or perform their work publicly, or grant the rights for another person to use the work. Creative works of literary, dramatic, artistic, and other intellectual property can be protected with a copyright.

An original work is protected under copyright law from the moment it is created. Although it is not necessary to place the copyright notice on the creative work, it is a good idea to do so, especially when publishing the work or putting it on display. This will help prevent a copyright

INTELLECTUAL PROPERTY

Intellectual property is any tangible or intangible property that is the result of the creative process. Creative works such as literary or artist works are considered intellectual property. Intellectual property can be protected by a copyright, trademark, or patent depending on the nature of the work.

- Copyrights protect original artistic or literary work.
- Trademarks protect works, phrases, or symbols that identify a company or product.
- Patents protect inventions.

infringement. All works within your portfolio or on display by any other means should have a copyright notice in an obvious place such as a lower corner of the work, the back of the work, or on any accompanying documentation.

Any work that was created after 1978 is protected under copyright law for the entire life of the author plus Seventy years. If there is more than one author, the copyright is protected for the entire life of the last surviving author plus Seventy years. In the case of a work made for hire, or anonymous and pseudonymous works, the copyright is protected for a term of ninety-five years from the year of first publication or 120 years from the first year of creation, whichever one comes first.

Creative works produced before January 1, 1978, were initially covered for twenty-eight years. A copyright owner could then file for a twenty-eight year extension. After the laws were revised in 1978, a sixty-seven year extension became automatic. However, an updated copyright certificate is not automatically issued. The copyright claimant must request the certificate with a renewal application and pay a fee. (There are several conditions and situations that can alter the copyright protection on creative works created prior to January 1, 1978. Further information is available at: *http://www.copyright.gov/laws/.*)

After a copyright expires, the work becomes **public domain**. Once a work is public domain, it is no longer covered under copyright law and is available for any individual or company to use without obtaining permission or paying any licensing fees to the former copyright holder.

9.1.1 Fair Use

Under certain circumstances a person may use another author's creative works protected under a copyright without permission or compensation to the original author. This is known as **fair use**. Examples of fair use include:

- Satire, parody, and caricatures
- Quotations used in commentary, review, and criticism

COPYRIGHT NOTICE

A copyright notice is signified by the word *copyright* or the symbol "©", followed by the name of the author or copyright owner (see: work-for-hire) and the year of completion of publication (For example, "© John Doe 2005" or "Copyright John Doe 2005.") You can insert the copyright symbol (©) on the Windows Operating Systems by using the shortcut keys, "ALT+0169" or within your word processor with the shortcut keys, "ALT+CTRL+C." On a Macintosh Operating System, use the shortcut keys, "Option+G."

- Quotation of a short passage in a scholarly or technical work to illustrate an author's ideas
- Summarization in a news report or article; may also include imagery
- A teacher or student making a reproduction of a small passage for a lesson
- Use in a court proceeding
- An image in the background of a newsreel or broadcast

The law is not always clear in what is considered fair use. When possible, always try to obtain permission. Just because a work may be unpublished does not mean it is not available under fair use. Some factors that will be considered if a use is considered "fair use" are:

1. The purpose and character of the use, including whether such use is of a commercial nature or is for nonprofit educational purposes;
2. The nature of the copyrighted work;
3. The amount and substantiality of the portion used in relation to the copyrighted work as a whole; and
4. The effect of the use upon the potential market for or value of the copyrighted work.[1]

9.2 WHAT CAN BE PROTECTED WITH A COPYRIGHT?

An idea is not copyrightable. In order to protect a creative work, it must be represented in a fixed form. Examples of fixed forms include manuscripts, paintings, illustrations, video recording, photographs, books, magazines, newspapers, and audio recordings. The categories for copyrightable works include:

1. Literary works
2. Musical works, including any accompanying words
3. Dramatic works, including any accompanying music
4. Pantomimes and choreographic works
5. Pictorial, graphic, and sculptural works

---

[1] Copyright Law of the United States of America and Related Laws Contained in Title 17 of the United States Code, Circular 92 (n.d.) Retrieved August 10, 2007, from http://www.copyright.gov/title17/92chap1.html#107

6. Motion pictures and other audiovisual works

7. Sound recordings

8. Architectural works

Copyright law excludes protection of an original work of authorship to any idea, procedure, process, system, method of operation, concept, principle, or discovery regardless of how an author describes, explains, illustrates, or embodies the work.[2]

9.3 WHO OWNS A COPYRIGHT?

The rightful claimant of a copyright can vary depending on the terms and conditions in which the work was created. The owner of the copyright is considered the author. Generally speaking, the author is the creator of the work. Only the author can transfer the ownership of the copyright.

The term *author* can be a confusing term. In the case of "work made for hire," the employer is considered the author. If an employee creates a work as a duty of his or her job, the employer owns the rights. An employer can list the employee's name on the copyright form, but is not obligated to do so. Under the author's section of the copyright form, the company will claim itself as the author, but can also include the employee's name (for example: "ABC Designing Co. employer for hire Anne Smith"). In this example, ABC Designing Co. is the owner of the copyright. Anne Smith is given credit, but does not have any legal rights to the creative work.

Depending on the contract, a freelancer who is commissioned to create a work may or may not have ownership claims to the work. If the contract states "work made for hire," then the contracting

---

WORK MADE FOR HIRE

Any work that is prepared by an employee as part of his job duties; or a work that is specially ordered, contracted, or commissioned as **"work made for hire"** is owned by the employer, company, or individual that is requesting the work. The employee or artist has no claim to the creative work. The employer owns all intellectual property rights to the work.

---

[2] Copyright Law of the United States of America and Related Laws Contained in Title 17 of the United States Code, Circular 92 (n.d.) Retrieved August 10, 2007, from http://www.copyright.gov/title17/92chap1.html#102

company or individual owns the creative work, not the freelancer. If freelancers do not want to sell their rights, they may choose to license the work exclusively or nonexclusively. The terms and time period of such a license can vary depending on what the needs are of the client and the designer.

When a creative work is contributed to a collective work (for example, an illustration used within a nationally published magazine), the original copyright owner retains ownership unless the author expressly transfers the rights. The owners of the compilation have only acquired the privilege to use and distribute the original work as part of their collective work. Terms of use should be outlined in writing before letting someone use your intellectual property as part of their collective work. Issues to address in a contract include payment (if any), form of presentation, right to alter the creative work, time period of use, and so on.

Copyright ownership can be transferred to another individual or corporation through a written agreement. The terms and compensation (if any) for transferring ownership is at the discretion of the parties participating in the transfer. It is a good idea to file an updated copyright form signifying the transfer with the U.S. Copyright Office. The transfer can be completed using the appropriate copyright form (See Table 9–1).

9.4 FILING A COPYRIGHT

The process of filing a copyright is simple. You will need a copy of the work you are copyrighting, the correct form, and $45 for the filing fee. Depending on what you want to copyright, different forms are required. Table 9–1 highlights which form should be used for different copyright types.

TABLE 9–1   Types of Copyright Forms

Form	Use of Form
PA (Performing Arts)	This form is used for any published or unpublished work that is prepared for the purpose of being "performed" directly before an audience or indirectly "by means of any device or process." Works of performing arts include: **(1) musical works, including any accompanying words; (2) dramatic works, including any accompanying music; (3) pantomimes and choreographic works; and (4) motion pictures and other audiovisual works**.

(continued)

TABLE 9–1 (continued)

Form	Use of Form
SE (Serial)	This form is used for registration of each individual issue of a serial work. Serial works include: **periodicals; newspapers; annuals; the journals, proceedings, transactions, and so on of societies**. This form is not to be used for an individual contribution to a serial publication. When copyrighting an individual contribution, use Form TX.
SR (Sound Recording)	This form is used for registration of published or unpublished **sound recordings**. *It is only used to copyright the sound recording itself.* It may also be used to simultaneously copyright the musical, dramatic, or literary work recorded on the phonorecord when the same claimant is filing the copyright. Do not use this form for copyrighting the audio portion of audiovisual works (motion picture soundtracks, audio recording accompanying a filmstrip, and so on); copyright audiovisuals with Form PA.
TX (Text)	This form is used for registration of published or unpublished *nondramatic literary works* such as **fiction, nonfiction, poetry, textbooks, reference works, directories, catalogs, advertising copy, compilations of information, and computer programs**.
VA (Visual Arts)	This form is used for registration of published or unpublished works of visual arts. Included in this class are **pictorial, graphic, or sculptural works**; including **two-dimensional and three-dimensional works of fine art, graphic art, applied art, photographs, prints, art reproductions, maps, globes, charts, technical drawings, diagrams, and models**.
G/DN (Group/daily newspapers and newsletters)	Use this form to copyright **all issues of a daily newspaper or newsletter for a given month**. The work must be a "work made for hire," and the author and copyright claimant must be the same person or organization.

Source: www.copyright.gov

The following Figures 9–1 and 9–2 are samples of a completed VA form.

Copyright Office fees are subject to change. For current fees, check the Copyright Office website at *www.copyright.gov*, write the Copyright Office, or call (202) 707-3000.

Form VA
For a Work of the Visual Arts
UNITED STATES COPYRIGHT OFFICE

REGISTRATION NUMBER

_____

VA   VAU
EFFECTIVE DATE OF REGISTRATION

Month   Day   Year

DO NOT WRITE ABOVE THIS LINE. IF YOU NEED MORE SPACE, USE A SEPARATE CONTINUATION SHEET.

1

Title of This Work ▼

Lagoon at Midnight

NATURE OF THIS WORK ▼ See instructions

Photograph

Previous or Alternative Titles ▼

Publication as a Contribution If this work was published as a contribution to a periodical, serial, or collection, give information about the collective work in which the contribution appeared. **Title of Collective Work ▼**

If published in a periodical or serial give: Volume ▼   Number ▼   Issue Date ▼   On Pages ▼

2

a

NAME OF AUTHOR ▼

Jane Doe

DATES OF BIRTH AND DEATH
Year Born ▼   Year Died ▼
1984

NOTE

Under the law, the "author" of a "work made for hire" is generally the employer, not the employee (see instructions). For any part of this work that was "made for hire" check "Yes" in the space provided, give the employer (or other person for whom the work was prepared) as "Author" of that part, and leave the space for dates of birth and death blank.

Was this contribution to the work a "work made for hire"?
☐ Yes
☒ No

Author's Nationality or Domicile
Name of Country
OR { Citizen of *United States of America*
Domiciled in _____

Was This Author's Contribution to the Work
Anonymous?   ☐ Yes ☒ No
Pseudonymous? ☐ Yes ☒ No
If the answer to either of these questions is "Yes," see detailed instructions.

Nature of Authorship Check appropriate box(es). **See instructions**
☐ 3-Dimensional sculpture   ☐ Map   ☐ Technical drawing
☐ 2-Dimensional artwork   ☒ Photograph   ☐ Text
☐ Reproduction of work of art   ☐ Jewelry design   ☐ Architectural work

b

Name of Author ▼

Dates of Birth and Death
Year Born ▼   Year Died ▼

Was this contribution to the work a "work made for hire"?
☐ Yes
☐ No

Author's Nationality or Domicile
Name of Country
OR { Citizen of _____
Domiciled in _____

Was This Author's Contribution to the Work
Anonymous?   ☐ Yes ☐ No
Pseudonymous? ☐ Yes ☐ No
If the answer to either of these questions is "Yes," see detailed instructions.

Nature of Authorship Check appropriate box(es). **See instructions**
☐ 3-Dimensional sculpture   ☐ Map   ☐ Technical drawing
☐ 2-Dimensional artwork   ☐ Photograph   ☐ Text
☐ Reproduction of work of art   ☐ Jewelry design   ☐ Architectural work

3

a

Year in Which Creation of This Work Was
Completed   *2005*   Year

This information must be given in all cases.

b

Date and Nation of First Publication of This Particular Work
Complete this information ONLY if this work has been published.
Month _____ Day _____ Year _____
Nation

4

See instructions before completing this space.

COPYRIGHT CLAIMANT(S) Name and address must be given even if the claimant is the same as the author given in space 2. ▼
Jane Doe
1234 4th Avenue
New York, NY 11121

Transfer If the claimant(s) named here in space 4 is (are) different from the author(s) named in space 2, give a brief statement of how the claimant(s) obtained ownership of the copyright. ▼

DO NOT WRITE HERE OFFICE USE ONLY

APPLICATION RECEIVED
_____
ONE DEPOSIT RECEIVED
_____
TWO DEPOSITS RECEIVED
_____
FUNDS RECEIVED

MORE ON BACK ▶ • Complete all applicable spaces (numbers 5-9) on the reverse side of this page.
• See detailed instructions.   • Sign the form at line 8.

DO NOT WRITE HERE
Page 1 of _____ pages

FIGURE 9–1

EXAMINED BY	**FORM VA**
CHECKED BY	
☐ CORRESPONDENCE Yes	FOR COPYRIGHT OFFICE USE ONLY

DO NOT WRITE ABOVE THIS LINE. IF YOU NEED MORE SPACE, USE A SEPARATE CONTINUATION SHEET.

PREVIOUS REGISTRATION Has registration for this work, or for an earlier version of this work, already been made in the Copyright Office?

☐ **Yes** ☐ **No** If your answer is "Yes," why is another registration being sought? (Check appropriate box.) ▼

a. ☐ This is the first published edition of a work previously registered in unpublished form.

b. ☐ This is the first application submitted by this author as copyright claimant.

c. ☐ This is a changed version of the work, as shown by space 6 on this application.

If your answer is "Yes," give: **Previous Registration Number** ▼ _____ **Year of Registration** ▼ _____

5

DERIVATIVE WORK OR COMPILATION Complete both space 6a and 6b for a derivative work; complete only 6b for a compilation.

a. Preexisting Material Identify any preexisting work or works that this work is based on or incorporates. ▼

b. Material Added to This Work Give a brief, general statement of the material that has been added to this work and in which copyright is claimed. ▼

6

a

b

See instructions
before completing
this space.

DEPOSIT ACCOUNT If the registration fee is to be charged to a Deposit Account established in the Copyright Office, give name and number of Account.

Name ▼ _____ **Account Number** ▼ _____

CORRESPONDENCE Give name and address to which correspondence about this application should be sent. Name/Address/Apt/City/State/Zip ▼

Jane Doe
1234 4th Avenue
New York, NY 11121

7

a

b

Area code and daytime telephone number (*212*) *555-1234*   Fax number ( )

Email *J_Doe@careercrib.com*

CERTIFICATION* I, the undersigned, hereby certify that I am the

check only one ▶ {
☒ author
☐ other copyright claimant
☐ owner of exclusive right(s)
☐ authorized agent of _____
Name of author or other copyright claimant, or owner of exclusive right(s) ▲

8

of the work identified in this application and that the statements made by me in this application are correct to the best of my knowledge.

Typed or printed name and date ▼ If this application gives a date of publication in space 3, do not sign and submit it before that date.

Jane Doe _____ Date *December 4, 2005*

Handwritten signature (X) ▼

x *Jane Doe*

Certificate will be mailed in window envelope to this address:	Name ▼ *Jane Doe* Number/Street/Apt ▼ *1234 4th Avenue* City/State/ZIP ▼ *New York, NY 11121*	**YOU MUST:** • Complete all necessary spaces • Sign your application in space 8 **SEND ALL 3 ELEMENTS** **IN THE SAME PACKAGE:** 1. Application form 2. Nonrefundable filing fee in check or money order payable to *Register of Copyrights* 3. Deposit material **MAIL TO:** Library of Congress Copyright Office 101 Independence Avenue SE Washington, DC 20559-6000

9

*17 *USC* §506(e): Any person who knowingly makes a false representation of a material fact in the application for copyright registration provided for by section 409, or in any written statement filed in connection with the application, shall be fined not more than $2,500.

Form VA   Rev: 07/2006   Print: 07/2006—30,000   Printed on recycled paper   U.S. Government Printing Office: 2004-320-958 / 60,126

FIGURE 9-2

The following examples are excerpted from the above completed VA form. Each figure is followed by an explanation of the information contained within the highlighted section.

⊙ Form VA
For a Work of the Visual Arts
UNITED STATES COPYRIGHT OFFICE

REGISTRATION NUMBER

VA   VAU

EFFECTIVE DATE OF REGISTRATION

Month   Day   Year

DO NOT WRITE ABOVE THIS LINE. IF YOU NEED MORE SPACE, USE A SEPARATE CONTINUATION SHEET.

1

Title of This Work ▼

Lagoon at Midnight

NATURE OF THIS WORK ▼ See instructions

Photograph

Previous or Alternative Titles ▼

Publication as a Contribution If this work was published as a contribution to a periodical, serial, or collection, give information about the collective work in which the contribution appeared. **Title of Collective Work ▼**

If published in a periodical or serial give: **Volume ▼**   **Number ▼**   **Issue Date ▼**   **On Pages ▼**

FIGURE 9-3

SPACE 1: Title (Figure 9–3)

Title of this work. A name must be given to identify the work you are copyrighting. This title will be used for indexing and identifying your creative work.

Publication as a contribution. Only use this line if the creative work is being used in a periodical, serial, or collection. In this line give the information for publication or collection that it will be included in.

Nature of this work. This line should include a brief description of the type of creative work; for example: photograph, audio recording, oil painting, blue print, fabric design, map, screenplay, music composition, and so on.

Previous or alternative titles. If the creative work has a different title that someone might search, list the alternate and previous titles in this line.

2

a

NAME OF AUTHOR ▼

Jane Doe

DATES OF BIRTH AND DEATH
Year Born ▼   Year Died ▼
1984

NOTE

Under the law, the "author" of a "work made for hire" is generally the employer, not the employee (see instructions). For any part of this work that was "made for hire" check "Yes" in the space provided, give the employer (or other person for whom the work was prepared) as "Author" of that part, and leave the space for dates of birth and death blank.

Was this contribution to the work a "work made for hire"?
☐ Yes
☒ No

Author's Nationality or Domicile
Name of Country
OR { Citizen of   *United States of America*
     { Domiciled in _____

Was This Author's Contribution to the Work
Anonymous?   ☐ Yes ☒ No
Pseudonymous?   ☐ Yes ☒ No
If the answer to either of these questions is "Yes," see detailed instructions.

Nature of Authorship Check appropriate box(es). **See instructions**
☐ 3-Dimensional sculpture   ☐ Map   ☐ Technical drawing
☐ 2-Dimensional artwork   ☒ Photograph   ☐ Text
☐ Reproduction of work of art ☐ Jewelry design   ☐ Architectural work

b

Name of Author ▼

Dates of Birth and Death
Year Born ▼   Year Died ▼

Was this contribution to the work a "work made for hire"?
☐ Yes
☐ No

Author's Nationality or Domicile
Name of Country
OR { Citizen of _____
     { Domiciled in _____

Was This Author's Contribution to the Work
Anonymous?   ☐ Yes ☐ No
Pseudonymous?   ☐ Yes ☐ No
If the answer to either of these questions is "Yes," see detailed instructions.

Nature of Authorship Check appropriate box(es). **See instructions**
☐ 3-Dimensional sculpture   ☐ Map   ☐ Technical drawing
☐ 2-Dimensional artwork   ☐ Photograph   ☐ Text
☐ Reproduction of work of art ☐ Jewelry design   ☐ Architectural work

FIGURE 9-4

169

SPACE 2: Author(s) (Figure 9–4)

Name of author. List the name of each author on its own line. You can request a continuation sheet if there are more than two authors. If the work is a "collective work," do not list all the authors. Instead, give the name of the author of the entire collective work. If this work was created as a "work made for hire," list the author as the employer. You may include the employee's name as the creator. (For example: "ABC Designing Co. employer for hire Anne Smith.")

Dates of birth and death. List the year of birth for the author. This is optional, but is a good idea to help identify the author. If the author is deceased, you must list the year of death. *If this work was created as a "work made for hire," leave the date of birth and death blank.*

Author's nationality or domicile. You must list the citizenship or domicile (legal residence) for each author.

Was this contribution to the work a "work made for hire"? Check "yes" or "no." (See term *work made for hire* in section 9.3.)

Was this author's contribution to the work anonymous or pseudonymous? Check "yes" or "no" for each category. An anonymous author is when the author is not identified for the work. If the author is anonymous, write "Anonymous" as the name of the author. A pseudonymous author is an author using a fake name. You may list the fictitious name on the author's name. (For example: "Henry Henderson, pseudonym.") If the author creates the work under a pseudonym, but his real name is known, list both. (For example: "Joseph Michaels, whose pseudonym is Henry Henderson.")

Nature of Authorship. Use this line to describe the nature of the contribution that each author added to the creative work. This line will vary depending on the form being used. On the previous VA form, the nature of authorship is predefined by specific categories. The filer just checks the appropriate box. Other forms will look for very specific wording. Examples are provided in Table 9–2. Word the nature of authorship carefully. If an author's role is not clearly defined, the form may be returned by the Library of Congress for clarification.

TABLE 9–2 Nature of Authorship Examples

Form	Nature of Authorship Examples
PA (Performing Arts)[3]	• Music • Song lyrics • Words and music • Drama

[3] Form SE (n.d). Retrieved August 10, 2008, from http://www.copyright.gov/forms/formpai.pdf

Form	Nature of Authorship Examples
SE (Serial)[4]	• Musical play • Choreography • Pantomime • Motion picture • Audiovisual work • Collective work • Authorship • Entire text • Entire text and/or illustrations • Editorial revision, compilation, plus additional new material
SR (Sound Recording)[5]	• Sound recording • Words • Music • Arrangement of music • Text
TX (Text)[6]	• Entire text • Coauthor of entire text • Computer program • Editorial revisions • Compilation and English translation • New text
VA (Visual Arts)[7]	• 3-Dimensional sculpture • 2-Dimensional artwork • Reproductions of works of art • Maps • Photographs • Jewelry design • Technical drawing • Text • Architectural works

SPACE 3: Creation and Publication (Figure 9–5)

Year in which creation of this work was completed. List the year in which the work was completed by the author. In the case of a work that

[4] Form SR (n.d). Retrieved August 10, 2008, from http://www.copyright.gov/forms/formsei.pdf
[5] Form TX (n.d). Retrieved August 10, 2008, from http://www.copyright.gov/forms/formsri.pdf
[6] Form VA (n.d). Retrieved August 10, 2008, from http://www.copyright.gov/forms/formtxi.pdf
[7] Form VA (n.d). Retrieved August 10, 2008, from http://www.copyright.gov/forms/formvai.pdf

3 a | Year in Which Creation of This Work Was Completed _2005_ Year | This information must be given in all cases. | b | Date and Nation of First Publication of This Particular Work Complete this information ONLY if this work has been published. | Month _____ Day _____ Year _____ | | Nation

FIGURE 9-5

is being created or revised from a previously registered creative work, use the year from the current version being filed.

Date and nation of first publication of this particular work. Only use this line if the work has been published.

PUBLICATION

"The distribution of copies or phonorecords of a work to the public by sale or other transfer of ownership, or by rental, lease, or lending; a work is also **"published"** if there has been an offering to distribute copies or phonorecords to a group of persons for purposes of further distribution, public performance, or public display."[8]

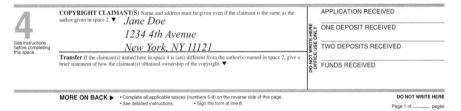

4 See instructions before completing this space. | **COPYRIGHT CLAIMANT(S)** Name and address must be given even if the claimant is the same as the author given in space 2. ▼ *Jane Doe* *1234 4th Avenue* *New York, NY 11121* | APPLICATION RECEIVED | ONE DEPOSIT RECEIVED | TWO DEPOSITS RECEIVED | FUNDS RECEIVED

Transfer If the claimant(s) named here in space 4 is (are) different from the author(s) named in space 2, give a brief statement of how the claimant(s) obtained ownership of the copyright. ▼

DO NOT WRITE HERE OFFICE USE ONLY

MORE ON BACK ▶ • Complete all applicable spaces (numbers 5-9) on the reverse side of this page. • See detailed instructions. • Sign the form at line 8.

DO NOT WRITE HERE
Page 1 of _____ pages

FIGURE 9-6

SPACE 4: Claimant(s) (Figure 9–6)

Copyright claimant(s). List the name of the person or company who owns or is claiming the copyright. This person can also be the same as the author or employer in a "work made for hire."

Transfer. If the author is not the copyright claimant, you must explain in this line how the claimant obtained ownership. (For example: "By written contract," "Transfer of all rights by author," "Assignment," or "by will.")[9]

---

[8] Form PA (n.d). Retrieved August 10, 2008, from http://www.copyright.gov/forms/formvai.pdf

[9] Form VA (n.d). Retrieved August 10, 2008, from http://www.copyright.gov/forms/formvai.pdf

EXAMINED BY	FORM VA
CHECKED BY	
☐ CORRESPONDENCE Yes	FOR COPYRIGHT OFFICE USE ONLY

DO NOT WRITE ABOVE THIS LINE. IF YOU NEED MORE SPACE, USE A SEPARATE CONTINUATION SHEET.

PREVIOUS REGISTRATION Has registration for this work, or for an earlier version of this work, already been made in the Copyright Office?

☐ **Yes** ☐ **No** If your answer is "Yes," why is another registration being sought? (Check appropriate box.) ▼

a. ☐ This is the first published edition of a work previously registered in unpublished form.

b. ☐ This is the first application submitted by this author as copyright claimant.

c. ☐ This is a changed version of the work, as shown by space 6 on this application.

If your answer is "Yes," give: **Previous Registration Number** ▼   **Year of Registration** ▼

5

FIGURE 9–7

SPACE 5: Previous Registration (Figure 9–7)

Check here if the creative work has been previously registered. If the work has been previously registered, check the appropriate box to explain why you are updating the copyright. Also list the previous registration number and year of registration. If this claim is a changed version of a previous work, then proceed to space 6 to explain what changes have been made to the work.

DERIVATIVE WORK OR COMPILATION Complete both space 6a and 6b for a derivative work; complete only 6b for a compilation.

a. Preexisting Material Identify any preexisting work or works that this work is based on or incorporates. ▼

a 6

See instructions before completing this space.

b. Material Added to This Work Give a brief, general statement of the material that has been added to this work and in which copyright is claimed. ▼

b

FIGURE 9–8

SPACE 6: Derivative Work or Compilation (Figure 9–8)

Only use this section if the creative work has been derived from pre-existing material and your creative work has added or changed the existing work.

Preexisting material. List the preexisting content that your current work has been derived from. (For example: Mona Lisa, Leonardo da Vinci). *Do not use this space if the current registration is a compilation.*

Material added to this work. Describe any additional new material that has been added to the preexisting work. (For example: "Adaptation of design and additional artistic work," "Reproduction of painting by photolithography," "Music arrangement," "Dramatization for television," etc.) In the case of a compilation, explain what the compilation is in this line. (For example: "Compilation of Renaissance Paintings.")

DEPOSIT ACCOUNT If the registration fee is to be charged to a Deposit Account established in the Copyright Office, give name and number of Account.
Name ▼   Account Number ▼

CORRESPONDENCE Give name and address to which correspondence about this application should be sent. Name/Address/Apt/City/State/Zip ▼

Jane Doe
1234 4th Avenue
New York, NY 11121

Area code and daytime telephone number (212)555-1234   Fax number (   )

Email J_Doe@careercrib.com

CERTIFICATION* I, the undersigned, hereby certify that I am the

check only one ▶
- ☒ author
- ☐ other copyright claimant
- ☐ owner of exclusive right(s)
- ☐ authorized agent of ___ Name of author or other copyright claimant, or owner of exclusive right(s) ▲

of the work identified in this application and that the statements made by me in this application are correct to the best of my knowledge.

Typed or printed name and date ▼ If this application gives a date of publication in space 3, do not sign and submit it before that date.

Jane Doe   Date December 4, 2005

Handwritten signature (X) ▼

x Jane Doe

Certificate will be mailed in window envelope to this address:

Name ▼ Jane Doe
Number/Street/Apt ▼ 1234 4th Avenue
City/State/ZIP ▼ New York, NY 11121

YOU MUST:
• Complete all necessary spaces
• Sign your application in space 8
SEND ALL 3 ELEMENTS IN THE SAME PACKAGE:
1. Application form
2. Nonrefundable filing fee in check or money order payable to Register of Copyrights
3. Deposit material
MAIL TO:
Library of Congress
Copyright Office
101 Independence Avenue SE
Washington, DC 20559-6000

*17 USC §506(e): Any person who knowingly makes a false representation of a material fact in the application for copyright registration provided for by section 409, or in any written statement filed in connection with the application, shall be fined not more than $2,500.

Form VA   Rev: 07/2006   Print: 07/2006—30,000   Printed on recycled paper   U.S. Government Printing Office: 2004-320-958 / 60,126

FIGURE 9–9

SPACE 7, 8, 9: Deposit Account, Correspondence, Certification (Figure 9–9)

Deposit account. Leave this space blank unless you have a deposit account already set up with the copyright office. If you do not have a deposit account (and you probably don't, unless you are working for a company that copyrights a lot of works), then send in a $30 check or money order with your application.

Correspondence. List the name, address, area code, telephone number, e-mail address, and fax number (if you have one) of the person who should be contacted about communication that may be necessary in the future.

Certification. You must date and sign this application. The signature must be handwritten by the rightful claimant, owner, or authorized agent.

Address for return of certificate. List the address where you want the certificate returned. *Make sure the address is legible.* This address will be used in the window of the envelope returning your copyright certificate to you.

MAILING YOUR COPYRIGHT

Send in the following elements to the Library of Congress, Copyright Office:

1. Application form
2. Nonrefundable filing fee in check or money order payable to Register of Copyrights. Do not send cash.
3. Deposit material. (A high quality copy or representation of your work.)

Mail to:

Library of Congress

Copyright Office

101 Independence Avenue, S.E.

Washington, D.C. 20559-6000

9.5 INTERNATIONAL COPYRIGHT

9.5.1 There Is No Such Thing as an International Copyright!

This is important to understand when making your creative works available. The Internet has made it much easier for people to steal your creative work and, depending on which country the thief resides in, you may not have any legal protection. That being said, you do have some protection in the international community. There are several agreements that have been made throughout the international community that provide some form of copyright protection outside the United States. The level of protection and the countries involved vary by agreement and member countries.

A complete list of countries that provide some international copyright protection and the agreements that they are a part of are available at: *http://www.copyright.gov/circs/circ38a.pdf*

9.5.2 Berne Convention

Before any formal international agreements, a creative work would have to be copyrighted in each individual country. If you filed a copyright in the

United States, that would not protect you in Spain. Copyright protection was only valid in the countries where an author had made a formal application. In addition, each country's protection would change based upon the individual nation's laws.

In 1886, a world convention was held in Berne, Germany, to address the issue of international copyright protection. At this convention, the international community drafted an agreement to extend automatic copyright protection to all the participating countries. A copyright owner does not need to register the work with an international organization; their protection is automatic among Berne Convention participating nations.

Under the **Berne Convention**, an author is protected for his or her entire life, plus fifty years. This is the minimum protection allowed by participating countries. Many countries provide longer terms. Both the United States and the European Union (EU) have extended the time period of coverage beyond the minimum life, plus fifty years. The EU and the United States provide coverage for Seventy years after the author's death. Publications and "work made for hire" are covered for ninety-five years from the first date of publication.

Initially the United States refused to join the Berne Convention. Adapting the standards within the Berne Convention would have required the United States to adapt new laws, especially in terms of moral rights. However, copyright law changes in 1978 brought U.S. laws much closer to the standards of the Berne Convention. Finally, after growing concerns of international copyright infringements, The United States officially adopted the standards and joined the Berne Convention effective on March 1, 1989.

> The Berne Convention is managed by the World Intellectual Property Organization (WIPO). The WIPO is located in Geneva, Switzerland. The WTO website is *http://www.wipo.int*

Members of the World Trade Organization (WTO) are required to abide by most of the Berne Convention's standards even if they are not a member of Berne. The Trade-Related Aspects of Intellectual Property Rights (TRIPs) is a comprehensive set of standards that require all WTO countries to extend copyright protection to all participating countries. As of October 27, 2005, there are 148 participating countries in the WTO.[10] (Further information about the World Trade Organization can be found at: *http://www.wto.org*)

---

[10] Understanding the WTO: The Organization. (n.d.). Retrieved August 10, 2007, from http://www.wto.org/english/thewto_e/whatis_e/tif_e/org6_e.htm

MORAL RIGHTS

Moral rights are an author's right to control if and how a creative work can be used or altered. The rights only extend to the original work, not reproductions, and protect the author regardless of who owns the copyright. Moral rights can be waived in writing, but cannot be transferred. Additionally, moral rights vary from country to country.

The Visual Artists Rights Act of 1990 (VARA) enacted in 1990 was the piece of legislation that defined moral rights to visual works. It was designed to provide visual artists with the same protection that was agreed upon in the Berne Convention. Under VARA, an author of fine arts and exhibition photographs has the right to claim or disclaim their authorship. An author also has some limited rights to prevent distortion, mutilation, or modification of their creative work. In certain cases, an artist may even have rights to prevent destruction of a work that is incorporated into a building.[11]

9.6 WHAT IS A TRADEMARK?

A Trademark is a protected intellectual property that identifies and distinguishes a company or product. It can be made of words, phrases, symbols, or designs. A service mark is essentially the same as a trademark, but it identifies the source of a service instead of the product. *The rules and protection are the same for both trademarks and service marks. In this section the term trademark refers to both.* (Examples of trademarks include the Yahoo yodel for Yahoo.com, the Mercedes Benz emblem, and the Nike swoosh.)

It is not necessary to register a mark to have it associated with your company or product, but it is to your advantage. Benefits include:

- Constructive notice to the public of the registrant's claim of ownership of the mark
- A legal presumption of the registrant's ownership of the mark and the registrant's exclusive right to use the mark nationwide on or in connection with the goods and/or services listed in the registration
- The ability to bring an action concerning the mark in federal court

---

[11] Waiver of Moral Rights in Visual Artworks (October 24, 1996). Retrieved August 10, 2008, from http://www.copyright.gov/reports/exsum.html

- The use of the U.S. registration as a basis to obtain registration in foreign countries
- The ability to file the U.S. registration with the U.S. Customs Service to prevent importation of infringing foreign goods.[12]

You do not need to file the trademark to make a claim of a trademark. Use the symbols "TM" (trademark) or "SM" (service mark) to show your claim of ownership. You can use these symbols regardless of whether you filed your trademark with the United States Patent and Trademark Office (USPTO). However, you can only use the "®" symbol when your trademark has been processed and accepted by the USPTO.

> The United States Patent and Trademark Office's website is: *http://www.uspto.gov.*

Filing a trademark is relatively easy and can be completed over the Internet or by mail. Additionally, the USPTO website allows a user to search existing trademarks. The steps to file are the following:

- Search existing trademarks to ensure availability of the mark you want to protect.
- Fill out the Trademark Electronic Application System (TEAS) form online or submit your application by mail to:

  Commissioner for Trademarks

  P.O. Box 1451

  Alexandria, VA 22313-1451

- The fee for electronic filing is $325 per class for the TEAS form or $275 for the TEAS Plus form.
- You are required to provide images of your trademark in a .jpg file format. Audio trademarks should be provided as a .wav or MP3 file.
- Confirmation of a pending application should be received within Twenty-four hours via e-mail.

9.7. ASSIGNMENT VS. LICENSING YOUR CREATIVE WORK

When allowing somebody to use your intellectual property for a fee, you have two options: assignment (sale of your rights) or **licensing** (granting permission to use your creative work. You still maintain

---

[12] Should I Register My Mark? (November 8, 2004). Retrieved August 10, 2008, from http://www.uspto.gov/web/offices/tac/doc/basic/register.htm

ownership of the intellectual property). It is very important that the language in the contract is clear. When negotiating an agreement, it is important to obtain the proper legal advice from a licensed attorney. If you do not understand the language in the contract, you could easily assign your rights instead of licensing them. (See section 9.8 for a more in-depth look at licensing.)

Assignment of your creative work means selling your rights to the work. Watch for terms such as buyout or work for hire.[13] These both refer to assignments of rights. The term *exclusive license* may be an assignment of your rights. In many cases you won't care if you are assigning your rights. This is especially true if you are being paid well or the work you are creating can only be useful to the company you are contracted with. You can also negotiate a return of your property if certain provisions are not met such as the company not publishing your work, not reaching certain sales figures, or after a certain time period. This is called a "reversionary right."[14]

In some cases of assignment, reversionary rights may be granted to the artist after a term limit or other agreement. A company may use an assignment instead of a license to have more control over the creative work for the time of the assignment which a license may not grant. In this case, the artist may have to pay fees for transferring the copyright, trademark, or patent back to the original artist.

9.8 LICENSING ARTWORK: NEGOTIATING AND MONITORING ROYALTY PAYMENTS

Reprint of *Licensing Artwork: Negotiating and Monitoring Royalty Payments*, by Attorney Richard Stim. NOLO, Berkeley, CA. *http://www.nolo.com/article.cfm/pg/1/objectId/C1A08DD9-4925-4138-8B54214F27C78F4C/catId/5DD3BD40-C970-45AC-BF68DC9BA717AFDB/310/238/181/ART/*. Used with permission.

For artists who have successfully licensed their works, royalty payments can provide welcome additional income. Be sure to understand how your royalties are calculated.

Whether you license a painting or jewelry, the benefits are the same. You retain legal ownership of the work—for example, you keep your

---

[13] Forst, Elizabeth. (March 2001). Know Your Rights (legal advice for photographers). In *Photo District News, 21,* p. 76. Retrieved August 07, 2007, from *InfoTrac OneFile via* Thomson Gale: http://find.galegroup.com/ips/infomark.do?&contentSet=IAC-Documents&type=retrieve&tabID=T003&prodId=IPS&docId=A72767969&source= gale&userGroup Name=lesaccess&version=1.0s

[14] Stim, Richard. *Should You License or Assign Your Art?* Nolo.com Retrived August 7, 2007, from http://www.nolo.com/article.cfm/pg/1/objectId/F661972E-290A-4E01-83926E1AF5BDF8C4/catId/5DD3BD40-C970-45AC-BF68DC9BA717AFDB/310/238/181/ART/

copyright or design patent—while someone else makes and sells your item (or duplicates your imagery on merchandise). In return for granting the license, you receive a *royalty*, a continuing payment based upon a percentage of the income from the licensed artwork. Imagine if, instead of laboring in your studio all day, you waited by the mailbox for royalty checks.

A. *Understanding Licensing Lingo*

The key to negotiating payments in a licensing deal is to understand the terminology. The following are some definitions.

ROYALTIES

A royalty is a fee paid to the creator of a work as a percentage of sales or for the rights to perform, display, or use the work.

Advance against royalties. An advance is an up-front payment to you, usually made at the time the license agreement is signed. An advance is almost always credited or "recouped" against future royalties, unless the agreement provides otherwise. It's as if the licensee is saying, "I expect you will earn at least $1,000 in royalties so I am going to advance you that sum at the time I sign the agreement." When you start earning royalties, the licensee (the company who licensed the artwork from the artist) keeps the first $1,000 to repay the advance to itself. If the artist doesn't earn the $1,000 in royalties, the licensee takes a loss. You don't have to return the advance unless you breach the agreement. On rare occasions, a licensee may pay you a "one-time license fee" at the time of signing the agreement. This fee differs from an advance because it is not deducted from royalties.

Gross sales. *Gross sales* refers to the total amount billed to customers who buy the product containing the licensed artwork. **Net sales** are usually defined as the licensee's gross sales minus certain deductions. In other words, the licensee calculates the total amount billed to customers and deducts certain items, such as the costs of goods, before calculating and paying the royalty.

Deductions. Deductions are items deducted from sales before the royalty is calculated. In general, it is acceptable for a licensee to deduct from gross sales any amounts paid for taxes, credits, returns, and quantity discounts made at the time of sale. It is also not unusual for a licensee to deduct shipping (the cost of getting the products to the buyer).

Deductions are as important as the royalty rate in determining how much money ultimately comes your way. For example, a royalty rate of 2 percent of net sales with no deductions may earn you more than you'd get from a 5 percent royalty rate from which various licensee expenses are deducted.

If possible, avoid deductions for bad debts and uncollectible accounts (that is, a third party orders products and then fails to pay), for sales commissions (a salesperson is paid a commission for each sale of the licensed product), for fees (a vague term that includes a wide range of licensee costs and business expenses), or for promotion, marketing, or advertising costs (these are costs of the licensee's business, not yours). If it's difficult to negotiate individual deductions with a licensee, consider setting a fixed percentage for deductions, say 10 percent.

B. *Computing Royalties*

Royalty payments are computed by multiplying the royalty rate against net sales. For example, a royalty rate of 5 percent multiplied by net sales of $1,000 equals a net sales royalty of $50. Royalty rates for licensing vary depending on the artwork involved. Below are some royalty estimates:

- Greeting cards and gift wrap: 2 percent to 5 percent
- Household items such as cups, sheets, and towels: 3 percent to 8 percent
- Fabrics, apparel (T-shirts, caps, decals): 2 percent to 10 percent
- Posters and prints: 10 percent or more
- Toys and dolls: 3 percent to 8 percent

In some cases, an artist may negotiate a "per unit royalty" that is tied to the number of units sold or manufactured, not to the total money earned by sales. For example, under a per unit royalty you might receive $0.50 for each licensed product sold or manufactured.

C. *Demanding a Guaranted Minimum*

If the licensee is very excited about your artwork and wants a long license, you may want to consider a "guaranteed minimum annual royalty payment" (GMAR). With a GMAR, the licensee promises to pay you a specific amount, usually at the beginning of every year, regardless of how well the merchandise sells during the year. At the end of that year, if the earned royalties exceed the GMAR, you're paid the difference. If the GMAR exceeds the earned royalties (you were paid more than the product earned), the licensee usually takes a loss (unless the licensee has negotiated to apply the difference to future GMARs).

D. *Auditing Royalties*

You'll want the right to perform an audit to detect and quantify a possible shortfall in your royalty payments. In your agreement, you should include an audit provision that describes when you (or your representative) can access licensee records, and that if the audit uncovers an error of a certain magnitude—commonly a sum between $500 to $2,000—the licensee will not only have to compensate you for the shortfall, but for the costs of the audit as well. You should also ask for an attorney fees provision in your licensing agreement so that in the event you must sue the licensee for royalties or audit costs, a court judgment would include your legal fees. Finally, it doesn't matter what royalty rates or other provisions you negotiate if the company you're dealing with is a crook. *Always* research the companies with whom you contract.

REVIEW QUESTIONS/ACTIVITIES

1. What protections did the Berne Convention create? How does this affect U.S. citizens?
2. Describe the difference between assignment and licensing of your intellectual property.
3. How does a trademark differ from a copyright?
4. What are moral rights?
5. When a designer enters into a contract as a "work made for hire," who owns the rights to the created work? Why?

INDEX